Donald Phillip Verene

The Philosophic Spirit
Its Meaning and Presence

STUDIES IN HISTORICAL PHILOSOPHY

Editor: Alexander Gungov
Consulting Editor: Donald Phillip Verene

ISSN 2629-0316

1   *Dustin Peone*
    Memory as Philosophy
    The Theory and Practice of Philosophical Recollection
    ISBN 978-3-8382-1336-1

2   *Raymond Barfield*
    The Poetic Apriori: Philosophical Imagination in a Meaningful Universe
    ISBN 978-3-8382-1350-7

3   *Jennifer Lobo Meeks*
    Allegory in Early Greek Philosophy
    ISBN 978-3-8382-1425-2

4   *Vanessa Freerks*
    Baudrillard with Nietzsche and Heidegger: Towards a Genealogical Analysis
    ISBN 978-3-8382-1474-0

5   *Thora Ilin Bayer and Donald Phillip Verene*
    Philosophical Ideas
    A Historical Study
    ISBN 978-3-8382-1585-3

6   *Jeffrey Andrew Barash*
    Shadows of Being
    Encounters with Heidegger in Political Theory and Historical Reflection
    ISBN 978-3-8382-1485-6

7   *Donald Phillip Verene*
    The Philosophic Spirit
    Its Meaning and Presence
    ISBN 978-3-8382-1781-9

Donald Phillip Verene

THE PHILOSOPHIC SPIRIT

Its Meaning and Presence

Bibliografische Information der Deutschen Nationalbibliothek
Die Deutsche Nationalbibliothek verzeichnet diese Publikation in der Deutschen Nationalbibliografie; detaillierte bibliografische Daten sind im Internet über http://dnb.d-nb.de abrufbar.

Bibliographic information published by the Deutsche Nationalbibliothek
Die Deutsche Nationalbibliothek lists this publication in the Deutsche Nationalbibliografie; detailed bibliographic data are available in the Internet at http://dnb.d-nb.de.

ISBN-13: 978-3-8382-1781-9
© *ibidem*-Verlag, Stuttgart 2023
Alle Rechte vorbehalten

Das Werk einschließlich aller seiner Teile ist urheberrechtlich geschützt. Jede Verwertung außerhalb der engen Grenzen des Urheberrechtsgesetzes ist ohne Zustimmung des Verlages unzulässig und strafbar. Dies gilt insbesondere für Vervielfältigungen, Übersetzungen, Mikroverfilmungen und elektronische Speicherformen sowie die Einspeicherung und Verarbeitung in elektronischen Systemen.

All rights reserved. No part of this publication may be reproduced, stored in or introduced into a retrieval system, or transmitted, in any form, or by any means (electronical, mechanical, photocopying, recording or otherwise) without the prior written permission of the publisher. Any person who does any unauthorized act in relation to this publication may be liable to criminal prosecution and civil claims for damages.

Printed in the EU

In memory of my friendship with the philosopher Ernesto Grassi (1902–1991) and our times in conversation at the Grassi's villa in several late summers on the island of Ischia, near Naples.

And thus it was from the Greeks
that philosophy took its rise.
Diogenes Laertius

Contents

Preface 11
Note on Interlinear Citations 17

Introduction: The Inscriptions at Delphi 19

Part One Beginnings 25
1. Hesiod's Muses 27
2. Thales of Miletus 31
3. Pythagoras of Samos 35
4. Empedocles of Agrigentum 39

Part Two Ancients 43
5. Socrates's Method 45
6. Plato's Quarrel 51
7. Aristotle's Ethics 57
8. Lucretius's Poem 63

Part Three Christians 67
9. Boethius's Consolation 69
10. Anselm's Argument 73
11. Cusanus's Learned Ignorance 77
12. Bruno's Infinite Worlds 81

Part Four Moderns 85
13. Descartes's Archimedean Point 87
14. Hobbes's Leviathan 91
15. Vico's Poetic Wisdom 95
16. Rousseau's Promethean Discourse 101
17. Kant's Schematism 107
18. Hegel's Speculative Sentence 113
19. Cassirer's Symbolic Forms 119
20. Whitehead's Actual Entities 125

Epilogue: Ancients and Moderns 131

Works Cited 137
Index 141

Preface

The philosophic spirit is part of the human spirit. Philosophy exists because we are mortal and because it is possible to pursue the rational imagination as a means to comprehend the meaning of our mortality. This pursuit has its beginnings in the ancient quest for self-knowledge, which includes the quest to know how to act as human. We are today in the fortunate position to look back over more than twenty-five centuries of this quest for self-knowledge. It is a way for us to face our own need to acquire self-knowledge and to fill our own need to grasp how to be human. There is nothing in the present as present that will provide self-knowledge. Self-knowledge presupposes memory that places the present in connection to the past. The future is always what emerges from the past.

The history of philosophy is part of the great theater of human memory. The figures of the philosophic spirit appear on its stage and put their ideas into words. And then, like the sequence of speeches in a theater, the moving finger of philosophy writes and, having writ, moves on. Memory holds all that there is. The reader of this small book is invited to enter into the ideas it records. My selection of the figures that hold these ideas is subjective. I do not intend them to be a master list. I intend them to be a philosophical miscellany, an album, taken from the history of philosophy, as the repository of the philosophic spirit.

My approach is that of *ars topica*, not *ars critica* — to appreciate what various philosophers have said as starting-points for thought, allowing the ideas they express to speak for themselves. In so doing, my aim is to follow Horace's advice, in his letter to the Pisos, known as *Ars poetica*, "either to instruct, or to delight, or to utter words both pleasing and helpful to life" (333-34). Philosophy shares with poetry these three possibilities.

I agree with Cicero, who said, in the *Tusculan Disputations*: "O philosophy, thou guide of life, o thou explorer of virtue and expeller of vice! Without thee what could have become not only of me but of the life of man altogether? Thou hast given birth to cities, thou hast called scattered human beings into the bond of social life, thou hast united them first of all in joint habitations, next in wedlock, then in the ties of common literature and speech, thou has discovered law, thou hast been the teacher of morality and order: to thee I fly for refuge, from thee I look for aid, to thee I entrust myself, as once in ample measure, so now wholly and entirely. Moreover one day well spent and in accordance with thy lessons is to be preferred to an eternity of error. Whose help then are we to use rather than thine? thou that hast freely granted us peacefulness of life and destroyed the dread of death" (5.2.5).

Philosophia is the transliteration of the Greek φιλοσοφια, which is formed by joining φιλια (*philia*, friendly love, affection, friendship, Lat. *amicitia*) with σοφια (*sophia*, wisdom, Lat. *sapientia*). Cicero says: "Wisdom [*sapientia*] is the knowledge [*scientia*] of things divine and human and acquaintance [*cognitio*] with the cause of each of them, with the result that wisdom copies what is divine" (*Tusc.* 4.26.57). Regarding friendship, Cicero says: "For friendship is nothing else than an accord in all things, human and divine, conjoined with mutual goodwill and affection, and I am inclined to think that, with the exception of wisdom, no better thing has been given to man by the immortal gods" (*Laelius on Friendship* 6.20).

The philosophic spirit arises from wonder (*thauma*). Wonder is produced when in our thought we arrive at an apparent equivalence between contrary meanings (*aporia*) such that we can see no way out. In Plato's *Theaetetus*, Theaetetus tells Socrates that he faces such *aporiai* when he attempts to think about fundamental questions of existence: "By the gods, Socrates, I am lost in wonder [*thauma*] when I think of all these things, and sometimes when I regard them it really makes my head swim." Socrates replies: "For this feeling of wonder shows that you are a philosopher, since wonder is the only beginning of philosophy, and he who said that Iris was the child of Thaumas made a good genealogy" (155c-d). Iris acts as the messenger of heaven and her father's name is a play on wonder.

Aristotle endorses this view of wonder when he says: "For it is owing to their wonder [*thauma*] that human beings both now begin and at first began to philosophize; they wondered originally at the obvious difficulties, then advanced little by little and stated difficulties about the greater matters" (*Metaphysics* 982b). *Thauma* is the middle term that joins *philia* with *sophia* and thus makes doing philosophy (*philosophein*) possible. The *aporiai* that are encountered by attempting to think about the nature of things induce wonder and cause those who encounter them to persist in the love of wisdom.

In Plato's *Symposium*, Socrates relates a speech made to him by Diotima, a woman from Mantinea, a village in the Peloponnesus, regarding the connection between Eros (Love) and wisdom. Diotima informs Socrates that Eros is by nature neither immortal or mortal, but is a figure midway between wisdom and ignorance. Diotima says: "In fact, you see, none of the gods loves wisdom or wants to become wise—for they are wise—and no one else who is wise already loves wisdom; on the other hand, no one who is ignorant will love wisdom either or want to become wise. For what's especially defective about being ignorant is that you are content with yourself, even though you're neither beautiful and good nor intelligent. If you don't think you need anything, of course you won't want what you don't think you need."

Socrates realizes that Diotima is describing the nature of the philosopher, who loves wisdom but does not claim to possess wisdom. Socrates asks: "In that case, Diotima, who *are* the people who love wisdom, if they are neither wise nor ignorant?" Diotima replies: "That's obvious. A child could tell you. Those who love wisdom fall in between those two extremes" (204a–b). Eros, as Diotima is speaking of him, is an ancient cosmogonic power. Hesiod, in the *Theogony*, says: "Eros, who is the most beautiful among the immortal gods, the limb-melter—he overpowers the mind and the thoughtful counsel of all the gods and of all the human beings in their breasts" (120–22). Diotima's characterization of Eros differs from Hesiod's. Diotima regards Eros as "neither immortal or mortal," but as occupying a position between gods and humans.

We can connect the sense of philosophy as *philia* (friendly love or affection), in relation to *sophia* (wisdom), with Diotima's comparison of the philosopher with Eros. That philosophy is a kind of *philia* is an epistemic claim. The philosopher does not claim to possess a particular kind of wisdom but to seek wisdom in the sense of an all-inclusive knowledge of things human and divine. In so doing, the philosopher stands between the human and the divine, as does Eros in Diotima's account. Diotima's claim is metaphysical. It speaks to the status of the philosopher's being. The philosopher's love of wisdom falls short of possessing wisdom, which is the province of the immortal gods. Yet the philosopher, in pursuing wisdom, is not following the life pursued by those human beings who have no need to seek wisdom itself and are content with knowing whatever they know. They do not realize that this is, in fact, a kind of ignorance. Once the philosopher realizes this sense of ignorance, the philosopher is in the position of Diotima's Eros—midway between the divine and the purely human.

Two tropes are necessary for the expression of philosophical thought— metaphor and irony. The trope that the philosopher shares with the poets is metaphor. Aristotle says: "The greatest thing by far is to be a master of metaphor. It is the one thing that cannot be learnt from others; and it is also a sign of genius" (*Poetics* 1459a). *Metapherein* is the ability to find similarity in dissimilars through the ingenious power of the imagination (*phantasia*). This ability is required to put forth *archai*, beginning points, for thought. The philosopher goes beyond the poet by adding irony to the narrative that the metaphor generates. Irony rests on the distinction between what *seems* and what *is*. To be a master of irony is to employ the question to induce dialectical thought—to consider what seemed to be settled on a subject in terms of the possibility of its opposite. Dialectic provides the means to confront *aporiai* and to continue philosophical thought.

The chapters that follow offer twenty concisely stated examples of the philosophic spirit from the ancient Greeks to Ernst Cassirer's philosophy of symbolic forms and A. N. Whitehead's speculative cosmology. Philosophy as the love of wisdom can be sought only through contemplation and a sense of what is held in cultural memory. It is one of the pleasures of the mind to enter into this memory and to re-discover what is preserved there that can be re-thought as part of the present. The past, then, illuminates both the present and the future.

We can learn to do philosophy by imitation (*mimēsis*) of examples. Aristotle says: "Imitation is natural to human beings, from childhood, one of the advantages over the lower animals being this, that human beings are the most imitative creatures in the world, and learn at first by imitation. And it is also natural for all to delight in works of imitation" (*Poetics* 1448b). Part of the definition of what is human is the ability to imitate. If then we find ourselves befriending wisdom, we can look to the examples offered us by those who have gone before us, and begin to think philosophically by imitating them.

I leave it to my readers to pursue the philosophic spirit in the wide range of recent philosophy—should they wish to do so. I agree with Frederick Copleston's concluding sentences in the seventh volume of *A History of Philosophy*: "There is no very good reason to suppose that we shall ever reach universal and lasting agreement even about the scope of philosophy. But if fundamental disagreements spring from the very nature of human beings themselves, we can hardly expect anything else but a dialectical movement, a recurrence of certain fundamental tendencies and attitudes in different historical shapes. This is what we have had hitherto, in spite of well-intentioned efforts to bring the process to a close. And it can hardly be called undue pessimism if one expects the continuation of the process in the future."

I thank Molly Black Verene for typing my handwritten manuscript and for her editorial skills. I thank Thora Ilin Bayer for acting as a first reader of the text and for valuable suggestions concerning various points of interpretation.

Note on Interlinear Citations

Plato — *Complete Works*. Edited by John M. Cooper. Indianapolis: Hackett, 1997. Cited by the standard "Stephanus numbers."

The Republic of Plato. Translated by Alan Bloom. New York: Basic Books, 1991. Cited by the standard "Stephanus numbers."

Aristotle — *The Complete Works: Revised Oxford Translation*. Edited by Jonathan Barnes. 2 vols. Princeton: Princeton University Press, 1984. Cited by the standard notation to Bekker's edition of the Greek text.

Aristotle's Nicomachean Ethics. Translated by Robert C. Bartlett and Susan D. Collins. Chicago: University of Chicago Press, 2011. Cited by the standard notation to Bekker's edition of the Greek text.

Classics — References to works of Greek and Latin classical literature are to volumes of the Loeb Classical Library, Harvard University Press, using standard forms of citation, with wording of quotations occasionally modified.

Diogenes Laertius *Lives of Eminent Philosophers*. 2 vols. Translated by R. D. Hicks. Cambridge: Harvard University Press, 2000. Cited by book and passage numbers.

Introduction: The Inscriptions at Delphi

In Plato's *Phaedrus,* Phaedrus and Socrates are walking along the banks of the Ilisus River. They come to a spot where, it is said, Boreas, the north wind, carried off Orithuia, daughter of Erechtheus, the Athenian king, while she was playing with Nymphs. Phaedrus asks Socrates if he believes this legend to be true. Socrates replies that he refrains from becoming involved in such considerations and that anyone who does so will become engaged in an endless task, "because after that he will have to go on and give a rational account of the form of the Hippocentaurs, and then of the Chimera; and a whole flood of Gorgons and Pegasuses and other monsters, in large numbers and absurd forms, will overwhelm him."

Socrates says to do so would take a great deal of time. "But I have no time for such things; and the reason, my friend, is this. I am still unable, as the Delphic inscription orders, to know myself; and it really seems to me ridiculous to look into other things before I have understood that. This is why I do not concern myself with them. I accept what is generally believed, and, as I was just saying, I look not into them but into my own self: Am I a beast more complicated and savage than Typhon [a fabulous multiform beast with a hundred heads resembling many different animal species], or am I a tamer, simpler animal with a share in a divine and gentle nature?" (229d–230a).

The inscription to which Socrates refers is the precept that appears on the pronaos of the Temple of Apollo at Delphi—*Gnothi seauton* (Know thyself). The entrant to the temple encounters this instruction, along with a second—*Mēden agan* (Nothing overmuch). Taken together, these two precepts, along with a third, offer a complete guide to human life. The first indicates the object to which thought should be directed. The second indicates the principle that should govern action—*sōphrosunē,* self-control, moderation.

Rarely cited is a third inscription, the single letter epsilon, or E. Is this inscription intended as a precept, to accompany the other two, and to stand alone as such? Or, is it the beginning of a word or phrase, the completion of which is lost, or was never made? There is no way to know what was intended. These inscriptions were said to be the work of the Seven Sages and were included in a list of maxims that comprised moral education and that were circulated to a number of Greek cities. The composition of the Seven Sages is given in various ways by various authorities. In the *Protagoras,* Plato lists "Thales of Miletus, Pittacus of Mytilene, Bias of Priene, our own Solon, Cleobulus of Lindus, Myson of Chen, and the seventh in the list, Chilon of Sparta" (343a). The list given in other accounts includes Periander, the tyrant of Corinth, who would replace Myson of Chen, in Plato's list. Myson was not a tyrant but was said to be the son of a tyrant. Thales is the only philosopher. The others are largely known for their political activity and for the laws they decreed.

The most famous attempt at treating the meaning of the Delphic epsilon is Plutarch's "The E at Delphi" that appears in his *Moralia.* Plutarch advances seven possible explanations of the Greek letter. Of its general status, Plutarch writes: "For the likelihood is that it was not by chance nor, as it were, by lot that this was the only letter that came to occupy first place with the god [Apollo] and attained the rank of a sacred offering and something worth seeing; but it is likely that those who, in the beginning, sought after knowledge of the god either discovered some peculiar and unusual potency in it or else used it as a token with reference to some other of the matters of the highest concern, and thus adopted it" (385A).

Apollo is the most Greek of all gods. With the Muses as his retinue, he is associated with the higher developments of civilization. In regard to ritual, especially ceremonies of purification, his oracles are the supreme authority. Delphi was the chief of his oracular shrines. It was to the Pythian at Delphi that Chaerephon, the friend of Socrates, went with his question of whether anyone was more wise than Socrates, as Socrates reports in the *Apology* (21a). Among the gods it was Apollo who most governed divination. Of Plutarch's seven interpretations of the E, the seventh is the most plausible. This interpretation holds that the E "is an address and salutation to the god, complete in itself, which by being spoken, brings who utters it to thoughts of the god's power." The E stands in a dialogical relation to anyone who is to enter the temple. Thus: "The god addresses each one of us as we approach him here with the words 'Know thyself,' as a form of welcome, which certainly is in no wise of less import than 'Hail'; and we in turn reply to him 'Thou art,' as rendering unto him a form of address which is truthful, free from deception, and the only one befitting him only, the assertion of Being" (392A).

"Thou art" as an assertion of Being makes the distinction between the ever-lasting permanence of the divine order and the contingent and ever-changing condition of human existence. Wisdom is to know and acknowledge the difference. E is placed beside *Gnothi seauton* to remind us of this difference. Thus: "We ought, as we pay Him reverence, to greet Him and to address Him with the words, 'Thou art'; or even, I vow, as did some of the men of old, 'Thou are One [*ei hen*]'" (393B). The two inscriptions express both an antithesis and an accord. Thus: "The one is an utterance addressed in awe and reverence to the god as existent through all eternity, the other is a reminder to mortal man of his own nature and the weaknesses that beset him" (394C). In this account the other precept, *Mēden agan*, is not mentioned. It is assumed as a way of acting toward the god and as a way of acting toward ourselves.

The significance of E as "Thou art" is endorsed by Giovanni Pico della Mirandola in his famous oration, *De hominis dignitate* [*On the Dignity of Man*] (1486), one of the key works of Renaissance philosophy. Pico says that the Delphic inscriptions are one of the things that compelled him to the study of philosophy. He regards "Nothing overmuch" as the standard for moral philosophy and "Know thyself" as including the pursuit of the investigation of all nature, as well as human nature. Pico concludes: "When we are finally lighted in this knowledge by natural philosophy, and nearest to God are uttering the theological greeting, *ei*, that is, 'Thou art,' we shall likewise in bliss be addressing the true Apollo on intimate terms."[1]

---

1 Pico della Mirandola, *Dignity of Man*, 235.

Pico's conception of the dignity of man is carried forward by the Spanish Humanist Juan Luis Vives in his *Fabula de homine (A Fable about Man)* (c. 1518). Vives says that "man is himself a fable and a play [*homo ipse ludus ac fabula est*]."[2] Vives's fable describes a banquet for the celebration of Juno's birthday at which Jupiter improvises an amphitheater in which he brings forth man on the stage as an archmime for the pleasure and enlightenment of the immortals who are the guests at the event. As Jupiter's mime, man appears and shows how human beings can be all things. "He would change himself so as to appear under the mask of a plant, acting a simple life without any power of sensation. Soon after, he withdrew and returned on the stage as a moral satirist, brought into the shapes of a thousand wild beasts. . . . After doing this, he was out of sight for a short time; then the curtain was drawn back and he returned a man, prudent, just, faithful, human, kindly, and friendly."[3]

Having been a plant, an animal, and a human, this actor reappears as having a divine nature. "The gods were not expecting to see him in more shapes when, behold, he was remade into one of their own race, surpassing the nature of man and relying entirely upon a very wise mind."[4] Then, to the delight of Jupiter, he impersonated Jupiter himself. Finally, "The whole man lay bare, showing the immortal gods his nature akin to theirs."[5] The gods were so impressed, that "he was received by them with respect and invited to the front seats. He sat in their company and watched the games which proceeded without interruption."[6]

The fact that human beings by their power of mind can make their own world through inventions, cities, customs, and ability with language makes them unique. "This one thing [mind], which is found in no other animal but man, shows his relationship to the gods. Of little good would all these inventions have been if there had not been added, as the treasury of all things and for the safekeeping of these divine riches, a memory, the storehouse of all

---

2 Vives, "Fable," 387.
3 Ibid., 389.
4 Ibid.
5 Ibid., 390.
6 Ibid., 393.

that we have enumerated."⁷ The human being unites the anima, the breath of life, the vital principle that is the soul, with the animus, the rational principle of its life.

The human spirit takes shape in culture. There are as many versions of what is human as there are cultures. Each culture has its origin in a form of mythopoeic thought. This thought supplies the culture with the archetypal images that become the basis of the ideas that comprise its inherent wisdom. Henri Frankfort and H. A. Frankfort, in "The Emancipation of Thought from Myth," distinguish the world of mythopoeic thought such as that found in the cultures of the ancient Near East from the thought found in the works of the early Greek philosophers. They observe that "in the systems of the Greeks, the human mind recognizes its own. It may take back what it created or change or develop it."⁸ This sense of thought is closed to the mythologies out of which pre-Socratic philosophy arises.

The Frankforts's account calls attention to Plato's comment in the *Timaeus*. Plato says that the observations of the earth and the heavens by the early philosophers "led to the invention of number, and has given us the idea of time and opened the path to inquiry into the nature of the universe. These pursuits have given us philosophy, a gift from the gods to the mortal race whose value neither has been nor ever will be surpassed" (47b). Plato explains that there is a kinship between the orbits of intelligence in the universe and the revolutions of our own understanding. He says: "So once we have come to know them and to share in the ability to make correct calculations according to nature, we should stabilize the straying revolutions within ourselves by imitating the completely unstraying revolutions of the god" (47c). In this way, philosophy can move the object of its vision from nature to human nature. Self-knowledge originates through this transformation. The Delphic precepts now become the basis of the love of wisdom.

Once this transformation is accomplished, these precepts can take us, as they did Pico, to the study of philosophy, and as they did Vives, to his instructive fable. These precepts provide the briefest and most profound guide to the philosophic spirit. We can

---

7   Ibid., 392.
8   Henri and H. A. Frankfort, "The Emancipation of Thought from Myth," 387.

say with confidence that all speculative philosophy is no more than the expansion of the ideas condensed in these three archaic inscriptions. We are taken back to them over and over. An example of this return is how Cassirer begins his *An Essay on Man* (1944), the title of which echoes Alexander Pope's line: "Know then thyself, presume not God to scan;/ The proper study of Mankind is Man."[9] Cassirer, as well as Pope, is using the word "man" in its first meaning, as given in the *Oxford English Dictionary*.: "A human being (irrespective of sex or age); L. *homo*."

Cassirer says: "That self-knowledge is the highest aim of philosophical inquiry appears to be generally acknowledged. In all the conflicts between the different philosophical schools this objective remained invariable and unshaken; it proved to be the Archimedean point, the fixed and immovable center, of all thought. Nor did the most sceptical thinkers deny the possibility and necessity of self-knowledge. . . . In the history of philosophy scepticism has very often been simply the counterpart of a resolute *humanism*. . . . We must try to break the chain connecting us with the outer world in order to enjoy our true freedom. 'La plus grande chose du monde c'est de scavoir être à soy,' writes Montaigne."[10] We might add Montaigne's statement: "Je m'estudie plus qu'autre subject. C'est ma metaphisique, c'est ma phisique."[11] For Montaigne, the greatest thing in the world is to be able to be oneself. To achieve this ability, Montaigne studies himself more than any other subject. He is both his physics and his metaphysics.

Both speculative philosophy and sceptical philosophy retain self-knowledge at the center of their thought. The memory of the Delphic precept becomes the hallmark of the philosophic spirit. This spirit takes us into the world of ideas, and these ideas, then, become our constant companions.

---

9 Pope, "An Essay on Man," Epistle II, 210.
10 Cassirer, *Essay*, 1.
11 Montaigne, *Essais*, 3:321.

Part One
Beginnings

1

Hesiod's Muses

Hesiod (c. 700 BC) and Homer (composition of the Homeric poems, 850–750 BC) are the first poets of ancient Greece. They are often cited together in Plato's *Dialogues* (e.g., *Republic* 377d, 600d, and *Ion* 531a–d). In the *Apology* Socrates comments on his death sentence by envisioning conversations he might have in Hades with those who have gone before him. He says: "What would one of you give to keep company with Orpheus and Musaeus, Hesiod and Homer?" (41a). Hesiod commences his *Theogony* by saying: "Let us begin to sing from the Heliconian Muses, who possess the great and holy mountain of Helicon and dance on their soft feet around the violet-dark fountain and the altar of Cronus's mighty son [Zeus]" (1). Homer begins his poems by calling upon the Muses. The *Iliad* opens with: "Rage—Goddess [*thea*], sing the rage of Peleus's son Achilles, . . . Begin, Muse, when the two first broke and clashed, Agamemnon lord of men and brilliant Achilles."[12] The *Odyssey* begins: "Sing to me of the man, Muse, the man of twists and turns driven time and again off course, once he had plundered the hallowed heights of Troy. . . . Launch out on his story, Muse [*thea*], daughter of Zeus, start where you will—sing for our time too."[13]

Hesiod reports the Muses as declaring: "We know how to say many false things similar to genuine ones, but we know, when we wish, how to proclaim true things" (*Theogony* 22). The Muses command the full range of speech—its power to mix the true and the false and also the power to speak only what is true. The Muses in their song tell of "what is and what will be and what was before, harmonizing in their sound" (35). The Muses place us in

---

12 Homer, *Iliad*, 77 (1.1-7).
13 Homer, *Odyssey*, 77 (1.1-10).

time and remind us that harmony is the principle that binds all things together. Harmony requires memory. Memory is the mother of the Muses. Their father is Zeus. Hesiod says: "Mnemosyne (Memory) bore them on Pieria, mingling in love with the father, Cronus's son—Mnemosyne, the protectress of the hills of Eleuther—as forgetfulness of evils and relief from anxieties" (53). The Muses teach us to remember, and with their power of harmony they allow us to pass beyond what is discordant.

The Muses are "the nine daughters born of great Zeus, Clio (Glorifying) and Euterpe (Well Delighting) and Thalia (Blooming) and Melpomene (Singing) and Terpsichore (Delighting in Dance) and Erato (Lovely) and Polyhymnia (Many Hymning) and Urania (Heavenly), and Calliope (Beautifully Voiced)—she is the greatest of them all, for she attends upon venerated kings too" (75).

The Muses inspire and provide kings with the ability to speak in accord with the wisdom of Zeus and thus with the means to rule in the manner of Zeus. Hesiod says: "Such is the holy gift of the Muses to human beings. For it is from the Muses and far-shooting Apollo that men are poets upon the earth and lyre-players, but it is from Zeus that they are kings; and that man is blessed, whomever the Muses love, for the speech flows sweet from his mouth" (93).

The Muses come to represent the arts of humanity and are differentiated according to their function. In late Roman times, Calliope is associated with heroic epic, Clio with history, Euterpe with flutes, Terpsichore with lyric poetry and dance, Erato with lyric poetry or hymns, Melpomene with tragedy, Thalia with comedy, Polyhymnia with mime, and Urania with astronomy. A museum is originally a place connected with the Muses. There was a museum in Plato's Academy and in Aristotle's Lyceum.

In the *Cratylus* Socrates says: "As for the Muses and music and poetry in general, they seem to have derived their name from their eager desire (*mōsthai*) to investigate and do philosophy" (406a). In the *Phaedrus*, Socrates and Phaedrus are sitting together in conversation, at midday. Above them they hear the sounds of cicadas. Socrates says the cicadas are engaged in conversation with each other and it is pleasing to them to see these two humans engaged in their own conversation. Socrates says: "They will be very pleased and immediately give us the gift from the gods they are able to give to mortals." Phaedrus asks: "What is this gift? I don't think I have heard of it." Socrates replies: "Everyone who loves the Muses should have heard of this."

Socrates then relates the nature of the gift. "The story goes that the cicadas used to be human beings who lived before the birth of the Muses. When the Muses were born and song was created for the first time, some of the people of that time were so overwhelmed with the pleasure of singing that they forgot to eat or drink; so they died without even realizing it. It is from them that the race of the cicadas came into being; and, as a gift from the Muses, they have no need of nourishment once they are born. Instead, they immediately burst into song, without food or drink, until it is time for them to die. After they die, they go to the Muses and tell each one of them which mortals have honored her. To Terpsichore they report those who have honored her by their devotion to the dance and thus make them dearer to her. To Erato, they report those who honored her by dedicating themselves to the affairs of love, and so too with other Muses, according to the activity that honors each. And to Calliope, the oldest among them, and Urania, the next after her, who preside over the heavens and all discourse, human and divine, and sing with the sweetest voice, they report those who honor their special kind of music by leading a philosophic life" (259b–d).

The philosophic life requires attention to all the activities that the Muses impart to humanity. Above all it requires harmonious speech, that is, coherent speech, the speech of the true that the Muses can produce when they will. The philosopher must, like the king, who follows Zeus, know how to use language properly, for philosophy exists through words. Socrates, in the final hours, talking with his friends before he drinks the hemlock, unexpectedly turns to Crito, the most devoted of his followers, and says: "For know you well, my dear Crito, that to express oneself badly is not only faulty as far as the language goes, but does some harm to the soul" (*Phaedo* 115e).

We must remember that the mother of the Muses is Mnemosyne. Without memory there is no possibility of self-knowledge because there is no self without memory and without memory there is no knowledge. In the *Theatetus* Socrates asks Theatetus to suppose that within us we have a block of wax. Socrates says: "We may look upon it, then, as a gift of Memory, the Mother of the Muses. We make impressions upon this of everything we wish to remember among the things we have seen or heard or thought of ourselves; we hold the wax under our perceptions and thoughts and take a stamp from them, in the way in which we take the imprints of signet rings. Whatever is impressed upon the wax we remember and know so long as the image remains in the wax; whatever is obliterated or cannot be impressed, we forget and do not know" (191d-e).

Philosophy depends on memory. The images stored in memory are the source of the imagination. The imagination is the power to bring forth what is in memory as though it were before the mind in perception. In this way, thought has content. Language is a theater of memory because all words have histories in the form of etymologies. To speak well requires a sense of memory as held in language, like the wax block of Socrates's example. Without the activity of the Muses there is no way to access memory, and without memory there is no way to pursue knowledge. Hesiod has made philosophy possible by bringing forth an account of the Muses and their relation to Mnemosyne.

2

Thales of Miletus

The history of philosophy begins with the pre-Socratics. The first of the pre-Socratics is Thales of Miletus (fl. c. 585 BC). The ancient city of Miletus, in Turkey, was one of the great cities of Asia Minor, having four harbors and a large trade. It was the most important of the twelve Ionian cities of Greece. As mentioned above, Thales was designated as one of the Seven Sages.

In the first book of *The Persian Wars*, Herodotus describes the war between the Lydians and the Medes, which had been going on for five years. He reports that: "They were still warring with equal success, when it chanced, at an encounter which happened in the sixth year, that during the battle the day was suddenly turned into night. Thales of Miletus had foretold this loss of daylight to the Ionians, fixing it within the year in which the change did indeed happen. So when the Lydians and Medes saw the day turned to night they ceased from fighting, and both were the more zealous to make peace" (1.74). It is certain that the eclipse did occur on May 28, 585 BC, but it is uncertain whether Thales had the means to predict it or to predict it with accuracy beyond the year in which it occurred. He did understand that the motions of heavenly bodies occur in cycles, and this understanding was likely the basis of his famous prediction.

As one of the Seven Sages, Thales is said by Diogenes Laertius to be the author of the Delphic precept of "Know thyself" — "To him belongs the proverb 'Know thyself,' which Antisthenes in his *Successions of Philosophers* attributes to Phemonoë, though admitting that it was appropriated by Chilon" (1.40). Chilon is also one of the Seven Sages. He was a Spartan ephor, worshipped as a hero at Sparta, mainly for his political services. When Thales was asked: "'What is difficult,' he replied, 'To know oneself.' 'What is easy?' 'To give advice to another.'

'What is most pleasant?' 'Success.' 'What is divine?' 'That which has neither beginning nor end'" (1.36).

Giambattista Vico claims that it is most likely that Solon was considered the author of "Know thyself" and that its original purpose was to encourage the plebeians in the first times of the aristocentric commonwealth of Athens to consider themselves equal to the nobles. Vico says: "Solon, however, had admonished the plebeians to reflect upon themselves and to realize that they were of like human nature with the nobles and should therefore be made equal with them in civil rights." Vico says: "Hence Solon was made the author of that celebrated saying 'Know thyself,' which, because of the great civil utility it had had for the Athenian people, was inscribed in all the public places of the city. Later the learned preferred to regard it as having been intended for what in fact it is, a great counsel respecting metaphysical and moral things, and because of it Solon was reputed a sage in esoteric wisdom and made prince of the Seven Sages of Greece."[14] Vico's interpretation is highly original, and it places the meaning of the famous precept in a new light. We might regard Thales as the original author and its attribution to Solon as a later claim, reflecting the political use which it acquired.

Most widely known and reported about Thales is the claim that all is water. The prominent source for this claim is Aristotle's discussion of the original causes advocated by his predecessors that he presents at the beginning of his *Metaphysics*. Aristotle says that not all of these thinkers agree on the number and nature of first principles. He says: "Thales, the founder of this school of philosophy, says the principle is water (for which reason he declared that the earth rests on water), getting the notion perhaps from seeing that the nutrient of all things is moist, and that heat itself is generated from the moist and kept alive by it (and that from which they come to be is a principle of all things)" (983b). Cicero endorses this view in *De natura deorum*: "Thales of Miletus, who was the first person to investigate these matters, said that

---

14 Vico, *New Science*, pars. 414–16.

water was the first principle of things, but that god is the mind that moulded all things out of water" (1.10.25).

Of the four elements—earth, air, fire, and water—water is dominant. Water dissolves earth; it is present in air in forms such as clouds, rain, and humidity, and it cancels fire. As Aristotle points out, all living things require water for their existence and water is the bearer of nutrients. The earth appears to sit on water because land is surrounded by water and when a well is dug, water is found to be below the earth. By claiming that the many come from the one, Thales puts forth the sense of causality inherent in the principle of ground-consequent. Water is thus the first cause, of which all other things are dependent. The pantheon of gods is an array of causes attached to various human activities and natural events that satisfy the imagination. But by employing reason attached to observation, Thales suggests that what is has a single intelligible cause.

Herodotus reports an instance of Thales's ability in practical matters. When Croesus, the king of Lydia, led his army against the Persians, he came to the river Halys and found no bridges or other way to cross it, "then Thales, being in the encampment, made the river, which flowed on the left hand, flow also on the right . . . so that, as soon as the river was thus divided into two, both channels could be forded" (1.75). Herodotus says this is the Greek account of this incident, but he does not believe it because he thinks there were already bridges there to cross the river. Whether or not the story is true, it reflects the Greek view of the cleverness of Thales.

An incident regarding Thales is told by Socrates in his dialogue with Theodorus in the *Theatetus*: "They say Thales was studying the stars, Theodorus, and gazing aloft, when he fell into a well; and a witty and amusing Thracian servant-girl made fun of him because, she said, he was wild to know about what was up in the sky but failed to see what was in front of him and under his feet. The same joke applies to all who spend their lives in philosophy. It really is true that the philosopher fails to see his next-door neighbor; he not only doesn't notice what he is doing; he scarcely knows whether he is a man or some other kind of creature." Socrates then adds: "The question he asks is, What is

Man? What actions and passions properly belong to human nature and distinguish it from all other beings? This is what he wants to know and concerns himself to investigate" (174a–b).

Aristotle, in the first book of the *Politics*, reports another story told of Thales: "There is the anecdote of Thales the Milesian and his financial scheme, which involves a principle of universal application, but it is attributed to him on account of his reputation for wisdom [*sophia*]. He was reproached for his poverty, which was supposed to show that philosophy was of no use. According to the story, he knew by his skill in the stars while it was yet winter that there would be a great harvest of olives in the coming year." Having this special knowledge, Thales leased all the olive presses that were available in the off season at a low price. When the unexpected great crop of olives came, Thales leased the presses back to their original owners at a significant profit. Aristotle says: "Thus he showed the world that philosophers can easily be rich if they like, but that their ambition is of another sort."

Aristotle comments that, in so doing, Thales "is supposed to have given a striking proof of his wisdom but, as I was saying, his scheme for getting wealth is of universal application, and is nothing but the creation of a monopoly" (1259a). Aristotle does not approve of this principle, but it is part of Thales's genius that he understood not only meteorology but also the economics of monopoly and was able to combine these two types of knowledge. The Thracian servant-girl is witty, but mistaken. Thales's *sophia*, acquired by his distance from the everyday sense of the world, allows him to be both in the world and out of it. Thales is the first to show this duality of the philosophic spirit.

3

Pythagoras of Samos

The name Pythagoras (c. 532 BC) is known to all who have studied geometry, from the Pythagorean theorem—that the square of the length of the hypotenuse of a right triangle equals the sum of the squares of the lengths of the other two sides. Pythagoras was born on the island of Samos, located off the west coast of Turkey, originally settled by Ionians and one of the principal commercial centers of Greece. Pythagoras made his home in Croton, in southern Italy, on the Gulf of Taranto, where he established a school and developed a Pythagorean community. In the *Republic*, Plato says: "It is told that Homer, while he was himself alive, was in private a leader in education for certain men who cherished him for his intercourse and handed down a certain Homeric way of life to those who came after, just as Pythagoras himself was particularly cherished for this reason, and his successors even now still give Pythagoras's name to a way of life that makes them seem somehow outstanding among men" (600b).

Pythagoras is said to have had a golden thigh. In his *Life of Pythagoras* Iamblichus says: "It is also a matter of common report that he showed his golden thigh to the Hyperborean Abaris, who said that he resembled the Apollo worshipped among the Hyperboreans, of whom Abaris was the priest; and that he had done this so that Abaris might be certified thereof, and that he was not deceived therein."[15] This same point of the divinity of Pythagoras is made by Porphyry in his *Life of Pythagoras*.[16] W. B. Yeats wrote:

> Plato thought nature but a spume that plays
> Upon a ghostly paradigm of things;

---

15 *Pythagorean Sourcebook*, 90–91.
16 Ibid., 128.

> Solider Aristotle played the taws
> Upon the bottom of a king of kings;
> World-famous golden-thighed Pythagoras
> Fingered upon a fiddle-stick or strings
> What a star sang and careless Muses heard:
> Old clothes upon old sticks to scare a bird.[17]

Pythagoras is said to have discovered the numerical ratios that determine the chief intervals of the musical scale, and in this way he was led to interpret the world as a whole through numbers. The "fiddle-stick" was the monochord with which Pythagoras experimented. The mathematical *harmonia* of the scale resulted in the conception of the "Music of the Spheres."

Pythagoras believed in metempsychosis and claimed to reach back in memory to former existences. Porphyry says that Pythagoras "taught that the soul is immortal, and that after death it transmigrates into other animated bodies. After certain specified periods, he said, the same events occur again, for nothing is entirely new; all animated bodies are kin, he taught, and should be considered as belonging to one great family. Pythagoras was the first one to introduce these teachings into Greece."[18] Porphyry indicates that Pythagoras conveyed this doctrine to wide audiences, including barbarians, among whom were magnates and kings. But, as Diogenes Laertius points out: "The Pythagoreans used to say that not all his doctrines were for all men to hear" (8.15). Porphyry says: "His utterances were of two kinds, plain or symbolical. His teaching was twofold: of his disciples some were called Students [or "knowers"] (*mathematikoi*), and others Hearers (*akousmatikoi*). The Students learned the fuller and more exactly elaborate reasons of science, while the Hearers heard only the summarized instructions of learning, without more detailed explanations."[19]

---

17   Yeats, "Among School Children," 48.
18   *Pythagorean Sourcebook*, 126.
19   Ibid., 130.

Pythagoras visited Phlius, the chief town of a small district of northeast Peloponnesus. The ruler of the Phliasians, Leon, spoke with Pythagoras and was impressed with him. The best account of their exchange is a passage in Cicero's *Tusculan Disputations*, which is based on a digression that occurs in a medical dialogue of Heraclides of Pontus, a prominent member of Plato's Academy. There is also a similar account by Diogenes Laertius. The original text of Heraclides is now lost, but the digression it contained is the source for the origin of the word "philosopher."

Cicero says that: "Leon after wondering at Pythagoras's ingenuity [*ingenium*] and eloquence [*eloquentia*] asked Pythagoras to name the art [*ars*] in which he put most reliance; but Pythagoras said that for his part he had no acquaintance with any art, but was a philosopher. Leon was astonished at the novelty of the term and asked who philosophers were and in what they differed from the rest of the world" (5.3.8). Cicero, writing in Latin, uses the word *ars* to represent what in the original Greek text of Heraclides was most likely *sophia*, used to produce a play on *sophia* and *philosophos*. Pythagoras is claiming that he possesses no particular skill or wisdom, but is a lover of wisdom, by coining the compound word *philosophos*. *Philo* generally designates the disposition of a person who is interested in or devoted to a certain activity.

Pythagoras explained that he regarded the life of humanity to be like the Great Games at Olympia, in which some came to compete and some came to engage in activity for profit in the buying and selling that accompanied the Games. But there was a third type, who "came for the sake of the spectacle and closely watched what was done and how it was done." Pythagoras claims: "So also we, as though we had come from some city to a kind of crowded festival, leaving in like fashion another life and nature of being, entered upon this life, and some were slaves of ambition, some of money; there were a special few who, counting all else as nothing, closely scanned the nature of things; these men gave themselves the name of lovers of wisdom (for that is the meaning of the word philosopher); and just as at the games the men of truest breeding looked on without any self-seeking, so in life the contemplation and discovery of nature far surpassed all other pursuits" (5.3.9).

Diogenes Laertius says that the first "to call himself a philosopher or lover of wisdom, was Pythagoras; for, said he, no man is wise, but God alone" (1.12). If we join this claim to Pythagoras's reply to Leon we see how clever Pythagoras was. Leon, as the absolute ruler of the Phliasians, is wise in the skill necessary to gain and hold political power. Should Pythagoras have claimed that he was in fact wise, taking the term *sophia* in a sense beyond that available to Leon, Pythagoras would have commanded a power comparable to that of the gods. He would have had a kind of superior wisdom that would place him in a precarious position of possessing a power beyond that held by Leon.

Instead, Pythagoras portrays himself as the *exclusus amator* of wisdom. He appears as interesting and novel, but harmless, occupying a position intermediate between possessing practical wisdom and divine wisdom. Pythagoras has the philosopher claim a role that allows the philosopher to move freely within the realm of those who hold political power. Because the philosopher knows that the life of the *polis* is not ultimate, the philosopher must wear the mask of the "lover of wisdom." This mask allows the philosopher freedom of thought and freedom of movement. The philosophic spirit is never entirely safe from the exercise of political power, but the philosopher knows the art of how to hide in plain sight. It is philosophic eloquence joined with ingenuity that makes philosophy possible and capable of persistence.

4

Empedocles of Agrigentum

Empedocles (c. 493–c. 433 BC) was born in Agrigentum (Greek, *Akragas*), near the southwest coast of Sicily. He is the author of two philosophical poems in hexameter—*Purifications* and *On Nature*.[20] In the proem of *Purifications*, Empedocles announces his divine status to the reader: "I greet you! I, who for you am an immortal god, no longer mortal." In *On Nature*, he announces: "You will learn; never has human intelligence soared further." Empedocles imagines a world-cycle that is governed by the two principles of Love and Strife. Love unites like with unlike and Strife divides by joining like with like. These two conditions alternately predominate. They form a natural dialectic within which we exist.

Empedocles replaces the view held by other pre-Socratics—that there is one universal substance from which the many derive—with the view that the four elements, earth, air, fire, and water, are mixed together to make the things of the world, as when painters mix colors to depict things in their paintings. In *On Nature* he says:

> As when painters color many-hued sacrificial
>   offerings,
> Both men [Empedocles is speaking of two particular painters],
>   by reason of their skill, very expert in their art,
> They grasp many-colored pigments in their
>   hands.
> Then, having mixed them in harmony, the ones
>   more, the others less,
> Out of these they compose forms similar to all
>   things,
> Creating trees, men, and women,
> Wild beasts and birds, water-nourished fish,

---

20 Laks and Most, eds., *Early Greek Philosophy*, 363–578.

> And long-lived gods, the greatest in honors:
> In this way may your mind not succumb to the
> error that it is from elsewhere [other than from the
> four elements]
> That comes the source of all the innumerable
> mortal things whose existence is evident,
> But know this exactly, once you have heard the
> word of a god.

Aristotle, in *On Sense and Sensible Objects* (437b26–438a3), quotes a central passage from the same poem of Empedocles, regarding a comparison between a lantern and the pupil of the eye:

> Just as when, thinking of setting forth, someone
> arms a lamp,
> A gleam of bright fire across the stormy night,
> Lighting [or, assembling] a lamp-case to protect it
> against all kinds of winds.
> Which scatters the breath of the blowing winds
> While the light, leaping outward as far as
> possible,
> Shines beyond the threshold with its unyielding
> rays—
> In the same way, the ancient fire, confined in
> membranes and delicate linens,
> Lay in wait for the round-eyed maiden [i.e., the
> opened pupil]:
> these protected it against the depth of water
> flowing around,
> While the fire gushed through outward as far as
> possible.[21]

In this passage Empedocles employs similes in order to accomplish a comparison between the lamp with its protective membranes and the pupil of the eye with its protective membranes. The lamp and the pupil have in common the presence of the primordial fire.

Empedocles moves from similes as found in Homer to similes as elements in a comparison. Homer's similes present no more than a likeness between two things. For example: "As fig

---

21 Ibid., 547; see also Snell, *Discovery of the Mind*, ch. 9.

juice quickly curdles milk, swiftly Apollo cured the wound of Ares (*Iliad* 5.902); "As a skillful man ensheathes silver with gold, Athena poured grace about the head and shoulders of Odysseus" (*Odyssey* 6.232). Similes of this type simply bring images together such that each illuminates the other. Empedocles's passage creates a comparison by making the lantern and the pupil of the eye instances of a third thing—fire. Empedocles accomplishes a *tertium comparationis*, that is, a formulation, which is the basis of class logic that Aristotle calls analytics. Aristotelian logic depends upon the ability of the mind to place one thing in relation to another within a class of which they both are members. This membership can be expressed in propositions. Propositions then can be deductively ordered to create syllogisms. In the *Poetics* Aristotle says: "Homer and Empedocles, however, have really nothing in common apart from their metre; so that, if the one is to be called a poet, the other should be termed a natural philosopher rather than a poet" (1447b).

As mentioned above, Empedocles declares himself to be "an immortal god, no longer mortal." His divinity is involved in the claim that he revived Panthea, a woman of Agrigentum who was in a coma for seven or more days and whose breathing had stopped. Physicians were unable to revive the woman, but Empedocles was able to do so because he took into account one factor the physicians neglected, namely, her soul, which Empedocles determined had temporarily left her body, illustrating that the treatment of disease is possible only if the physician understands human nature as a whole. There is no account, however, of how Empedocles accomplished the return of the woman's soul to her body.

In the *Phaedrus* Socrates speaks to Phaedrus of the art of healing as similar to the art of rhetoric. He says: "In both cases we need to determine the nature of something—of the body in medicine, of the soul in rhetoric. . . . Do you think, then, that it is possible to reach a serious knowledge of the nature of the soul without knowing the nature of the world as a whole?" Phaedrus replies: "Well, if we're to listen to Hippocrates, Asclepius's descendant, we cannot know the nature of the body either, if we do not follow that method" (270b-c).

There was an elaborate banquet held to honor Empedocles and to celebrate his medical achievement, involving perhaps eighty guests. Diogenes Laertius reports that, according to Hippobotus (fl. late 3rd. c. BC), when the banquet was concluded Empedocles got up and set out on his way to the volcano on Mt. Etna (on the gulf of Catania) and "then, when he had reached it, he plunged into the fiery crater and disappeared, his intention being to confirm the report that he had become a god. Afterwards the truth was known, because one of his slippers was thrown up in the flames; it had been his custom to wear slippers of bronze" (8.69).

Diogenes relates a second account of the banquet of Empedocles, as given by Heraclides of Pontus. This account states that after the banquet there was a sacrifice in the field of Peisianax, attended by some of the guests at the banquet. Following the ceremony many of the company dispersed and some retired to an adjoining field to rest under the trees, "while Empedocles himself remained on the spot where he had reclined at table. At daybreak all got up, and he was the only one missing. A search was made, and they questioned the servants, who said they did not know where he was. Thereupon someone said that in the middle of the night he heard an exceedingly loud voice calling Empedocles. Then he got up and beheld a light in the heavens and a glitter of lamps, but nothing else. His hearers were amazed at what had occurred, and Pausanias came down and sent people to search for him. But later he bade them take no further trouble, for things beyond expectation had happened to him, and it was their duty to sacrifice to him since he was now a god" (8.68).

The two stories, although differing in details, agree that Empedocles disappeared. In the *Phaedo* Socrates says: "No one may join the company of the gods who has not practiced philosophy and is not completely pure when he departs from life. No one but the lover of learning" (82b–c). In the *Nicomachean Ethics* Aristotle says: "So for one who is living, when his acting is taken away, and, still more, his making something, what remains except contemplation [*theōria*]? As a result, the activity of the god, because it is superior in blessedness, would be contemplative" (1178b). Empedocles's two poems were his preparation for his apotheosis.

Part Two
Ancients

5

Socrates's Method

Diogenes Laertius says: "Socrates [469–399 BC] was the son of Sophroniscus, a sculptor, and of Phaenarete, a midwife, as we read in the *Theaetetus* of Plato; he was a citizen of Athens and belonged to the deme Alopece" (2.18.). "He was a man of great independence and dignity of character" (2.24). There is no record of Socrates having a profession. At age seventy, Socrates was charged with "refusing to recognize the gods recognized by the state, and of introducing other new divinities," and by so doing, "corrupting the youth" (2.40). He was found guilty, sentenced to death, and imprisoned. In accordance with Athenian law and by order of the *thesmothetai*, the officials concerned with the administration of justice, he was required to take his own life by drinking hemlock (*conium maculatum*).[22]

Cicero says: "Socrates was the first to call philosophy down from the heavens and set her in the cities of men and bring her also into their homes and compel her to ask questions about life and morality and things good and evil" (*Tusc.* 5.4.10–11). Cicero's claim is reflected in Plato's *Phaedo*, which opens with Phaedo stopping at Phlius on his way back home to Elis, after having been with Socrates on the day of his death. Phaedo is speaking to a group of Pythagoreans who have settled in Phlius. Echecrates asks Phaedo: "Were you with Socrates yourself, Phaedo, on the day when he drank the poison in prison, or did someone else tell you about it?" Phaedo replies: "I was there myself, Echecrates." Echecrates asks: "What are the things he said before he died? And how did he die? I should be glad to hear this. Hardly anyone from Phlius visits Athens nowadays, nor has any stranger come from Athens for some time who could give us a clear account of what

---

22   Bloch, "Hemlock Poisoning," 265.

happened, except that he drank the poison and died, but nothing more" (57a–b).

Phaedo reports the extended conversation Socrates had with the Pythagoreans Simmias and Cebes in his prison cell, on the immortality of the soul. Well into this exchange Socrates, speaking to Simmias, gives his definition of the true philosopher, saying *"hoi orthōs philosophountes apothnēskein meletōsi* [those who rightly philosophize are practicing to die]" (67e 3–4). It is not by accident that Plato sets this dialogue in Phlius, where Pythagoras first coined the word "philosopher" and described the philosopher as a spectator of the world. Socrates transposes the role of the philosopher from spectator of the world to actor in the world.

Philosophy is that which can provide us with the means to confront our mortality and prepare us for death. Socrates says we cannot know what will occur after death, but we can assume that no harm can come to a good human being. A good human being, Socrates claims, is someone who, like himself, has not willfully made anyone the worse for knowing him. Xenophon, in his *Memorabilia*, describes Socrates's typical day: "Socrates lived ever in the open; for early in the morning he went to the public promenades and training-grounds; in the forenoon he was seen in the market [*agora*]; and the rest of the day he passed just where most people were to be met: he was generally talking, and anyone might listen. Yet none ever knew him to offend against piety and religion in deed or word. He did not even discuss that topic so favored by other talkers, 'the Nature of the Universe': and avoided speculation on the so-called 'Cosmos' of the Deep Thinkers, how it works, and on the laws that govern the phenomena of the heavens: indeed he would argue that to trouble one's mind with such problems is sheer folly" (1.1.10–12).

Socrates's method of talk was the elenchus (Greek, *elenchos*). The elenchus is a method of cross-examination, from *elenchein*, to shame. Cicero incorporates this form of reasoning in his *Tusculan Disputations*. Cicero says: "The procedure was that, after the would-be listener had expressed his view, I opposed it. This, as you know, is the old Socratic method of arguing against your adversary's position; for Socrates thought that in this way the probable truth was most readily discovered" (1.4.8). Cicero was an expert in arguing in the law courts. A maxim in cross-examination in a trial is never to ask a question to which the questioner does not already know the answer. Socrates knows the answers to the questions he asks, in that he knows what the person will say as an answer. But he does not claim to know the answer to the real question within his questions, namely — what does it mean to be a human being?

In the *Apology* Socrates makes the most famous statement to be found in the history of philosophy: "The unexamined life is not fit for a human being to live [*ho de anexetastos bios ou biōtos anthrōpō*]" (38a 6–7). The term "unexamined," although to be found widely in English translations of the *Apology*, does not accord well with Socrates's practice of elenchus. The entry for *anexetastos* in Liddell and Scott's *Greek-English Lexicon* gives its meaning as "without inquiry or investigation," and gives Plato's *Apology* as its source.[23] To "inquire," from Latin *inquirere*, is to seek to know by asking or questioning. To "examine" is to consider or analyze whether something given is true or not. To inquire is a more fundamental act of thought than to examine, and is that on which the process of examination is based.

It has often been thought that Socrates is urging his listeners to look into their lives and evaluate what they find, to introspect. The purpose of Socrates's questioning is not to introspect but to pursue the Delphic precept of "Know thyself." In Socrates's view we can pursue this precept only by talking with others. In so doing we come to know that we do not know. We experience the irony that is brought on by this Socratic principle of ignorance. The acceptance of this ignorance gives us access to that most Greek of virtues, *sōphrosunē*, moderation. *Sōphrosunē* comes from the discovery that we are neither a god and immortal nor an animal, unaware of our mortality. As human beings we find we can say what we are not, but we cannot say what we are. Human

---

23 Liddell and Scott, *Lexicon*, 133.

beings are the only beings that find the fact that they exist to be a problem.

Socrates's elenchus induces a sense of shame that we can do no better than affirm this discovery. Although elenchus leads us from argument to counterargument, Socrates says we should not become misologists: "'Let's not become misologists,' Socrates said, 'like those who become misanthropists, since we couldn't undergo a greater mishap,' he said, 'than hating arguments. Misology and misanthropy originate from the same practice" (*Phaedo* 89d). Misanthropy results from trusting others only to be taken advantage of by them. Because this disappointment occurs in some cases we should not abandon all humanity. Although we are disappointed that the elenchus does not produce an answer to our question, we are the better for having engaged in it. Our thought is improved, and we become more modest in regard to our position in the world.

Our soul while alive is attached to the body, and as such it is bound to the oscillation of pleasure and pain. This movement between pleasure and pain can be overcome only by the cultivation of the love of learning that takes place in the soul. This love of learning is essential to philosophy. Socrates says: "The soul of a philosophic human being would reason it out in this way: and it wouldn't think that philosophy is obliged to set it free, yet that when philosophy has freed it, it should of its own accord hand itself back to pleasure and pain and bind itself up with them again and carry out a never-ending task of a Penelope working away in reverse at some kind of loom [see *Odyssey* 2.92–105]. Rather, in bringing about a respite from these emotions, following reason and being always engaged in it, contemplating the truth, the divine and not what is based on opinion, and being nourished by it, it believes it must live in this way as long as it lives, and when it dies and reaches what is akin to it and of like nature, be rid of human evils" (*Phaedo* 84a–b).

In the *Apology* Socrates says: "What has caused my reputation is none other than a certain kind of wisdom. What kind of wisdom? Human wisdom, perhaps. It may be that I really possess this" (20d). An illustration of Socrates's kind of wisdom is the elenchus in which Socrates engages Euthyphro, near the king-archon's court, while awaiting trial. Euthyphro is a professional priest; he regards himself as an expert in the knowledge and performance of correct ritual in prayer and sacrifice relating to the gods. Thus Euthyphro can be expected to understand the meaning of *hosion*, the sense of holiness or piety required for proper relation to the gods. At the beginning of their conversation, Euthyphro says: "I should be of no use, Socrates, and Euthyphro would not be superior to the majority of men, if I did not have accurate knowledge of all such things" (*Euthyphro* 4e–5a).

Euthyphro says: "Something that the gods love is holy [*prosphiles tois theois*] and what they do not love is unholy [*mē prosphiles tois theois*]" (7a). Continuing the elenchus, Socrates asks: "Is the holy loved by the gods because it is holy, or is it holy because it is loved?" (10a). Euthyphro says that whatever he proposes, Socrates seems to make it go around in circles. Socrates replies: "What you're saying, Euthyphro, sounds like the work of my ancestor Daedalus" (11b–c). Socrates appears to make their arguments move about, like Daedelus's statues. Socrates says: "My friend, it seems that I've become much cleverer in my art than that man to the extent that while he only made his own creations not stay still, it seems I make other people's do so in addition to my own. And indeed, this is the real beauty about my skill, that I'm wise despite myself" (11d). Euthyphro is unable to stabilize the argument and breaks off the exchange, saying: "You see I'm in a hurry to go somewhere right now, and it's time for me to leave" (15e).

Socrates's philosophy is his method. His wisdom is his skill to create the elenchus. He has no doctrine to teach beyond the pursuit of the question. But in teaching us how to ask questions he has bequeathed to us the wisdom needed to engage in the love of wisdom. The asking of questions is an art distinctive to human beings.

6

Plato's Quarrel

Diogenes Laertius says: "Plato [c. 429–347 BC] was the son of Ariston and a citizen of Athens. His mother was Perictione (or Potone), who traced back her descent to Solon. . . . Plato was in the sixth generation from Solon. And Solon traced his descent to Neleus and Poseidon" (3.1). Plato founded his famous school possibly as early as 385 BC, at a site sacred to the minor hero Academus (or Hecademus), about a mile outside the wall of Athens. Plato's leadership and lectures in this school, as well as his writings, were his primary occupation for the remaining forty years of his life. Plato made three trips to Sicily, to Syracuse. His second trip involved his famous unsuccessful attempt to realize the ideal of the philosopher–king in its ruler, Dionysius II.

From the time of Pythagoras to the Platonic Socrates, the Greek world had not resolved the question of whether the sayings and writings of the *philosophoi* were a new kind of poetry or whether they embodied a new kind of knowledge. Were the thoughts resulting from the philosopher's love of wisdom to be regarded as an extension of Homer, whose wisdom was conveyed through the recitations of the rhapsodes? Or were these speculations of the philosophers to take their audience into another sense of things? This is a question Plato decides to answer before he concludes the *Republic*.

The *Republic* is a city in speech, an ideal city. In the *Laws* Plato says of such a state: "It may be that gods or a number of the children of gods inhabit this kind of state: if so the life they live there, observing these rules, is a happy one indeed. And so men need look no further for their ideal: they should keep this state in view and try to find the one that most nearly resembles it" (739d–e). In the *Republic* Plato says that one of the first rules of this ideal state is: "We must supervise the maker of tales; and if they make a fine tale, it must be approved, but if it's not, it must be rejected.

We'll persuade nurses and mothers to tell the approved tales to their children and to shape their souls with tales more than their bodies with hands" (377b–c).

It concerns Plato that poetic imitation (*mimēsis*) does not contain principles to determine what is worth imitating. Imitation implies approval and is thus inherently ethical. What is ethical depends upon a judgment of approbation or disapprobation. But poets make images for the sake of making images. In the third book of the *Republic*, Socrates says: "If a man who is able by wisdom to become every sort of thing and to imitate all things should come to our city, wishing to make a display of himself and his poems, we would fall on our knees before him as a man sacred, wonderful, and pleasing; but we would say that there is no such man among us in the city, nor is it lawful [*themis*] for such a man to be born there. We would send him to another city, with myrrh poured over his head and crowned with wool, while we ourselves would use a more austere and less pleasing poet and teller of tales for the sake of benefit, and who would imitate the style of the decent man" (398a–b).

Plato was originally a writer of lyrics, dithyrambs, and tragedies. According to Diogenes Laertius, when Plato "was about to compete for the prize with a tragedy, he listened to Socrates in front of the theatre of Dionysus, and then consigned his poems to the flames. . . . From that time onward, having reached his twentieth year (so it is said), he was the pupil of Socrates" (3.5–6). Plato turned his poetic ability into his dialogues and brought the Socratic elenchus together with the retelling of myths introduced by Socrates as "likely stories" that supplement argument or *logos* with *mythos*. In the ideal state, poetry is to act in concert with philosophy. Plato never gives up his love of poetry but incorporates it into his love of wisdom.

In the tenth book of the *Republic*, the question of poetry is revisited. The Platonic Socrates says that it was Homer who educated Greece, and that the charm of Homer remains. What, then, is the distinction between philosophy and poetry? The moral critique of poetry—that it is unable to teach virtue because of its indiscriminate attachment to, and portrayal of, the emotions—

must have an epistemic and metaphysical basis if this critique is to be more than just a doctrine of political prudence for the ideal state. The Platonic Socrates says that the poets were sent away from the city because: "The argument determined us. Let us further say to it, lest it convict us for a certain harshness and rusticity, that there is an old quarrel between philosophy and poetry" (607b).

This old quarrel is described in the *Laws* as originating with how the pre-Socratic naturalistic views of the order of the universe and the motion of heavenly bodies were regarded. It was thought "that if a man goes in for such things as astronomy and the essential associated disciplines, and sees events apparently happening by necessity rather than because they are directed by the intention of a benevolent will, he'll turn into an atheist." These early philosophers "concluded from the evidence of their eyes that all the bodies that move across the heavens were mere collections of stone and earth and many other kinds of inanimate matter — inanimate matter which nevertheless initiated a chain of causation responsible for all the order in the universe." These early philosophers were the first physicists. But, "these views brought down on the philosophers's heads a great many accusations of atheism, and provoked a lot of hostility; poets, in particular, joined in the chorus of abuse and among other inanities compared the philosophers to bitches baying at the moon" (967a-c).

The quarrel with the poets, as present in the *Republic*, depends upon two senses of vision. The poet sees with the bodily eye. What the poet sees are images. These images are made or imitated in words. *Eidos* remains, for the poet, what it meant for Homer—"What one sees," the appearance or shape, namely, of the body—a meaning that persisted in pre-Socratic philosophy. In Platonic philosophy, *eidos* is what is seen by the mind's eye. The words of the poet make what one can see with the bodily eye. The words of the philosopher make us see the unseen, with the mind's eye. The basis of the quarrel is that both poetry and philosophy are nothing but words. The poet and the philosopher are both imitators. The words of the poet imitate what can be seen. The words of the philosopher imitate the unseen. They imitate not what appears, but what is. What is are the *eidē*, the forms that are not seen except by the mind's eye. These forms make it possible to apprehend sensible things, but these forms are not themselves sensible. We must already have in mind the form of a thing in order to know what we are sensing.

The Platonic Socrates says that poetry can be reinstated if the poets or the protectors of poetry can produce an apology, a defense speech, in its favor, either in meter or in prose. "But as long as it's not able to make its apology, when we listen to it [to poetry], we'll chant this argument we are making to ourselves as a countercharm, taking care against falling back again into this love [of poetry], which is childish and belongs to the many. We are, at all events, aware that such poetry mustn't be taken seriously as a serious thing laying hold of truth, but that the man who hears it must be careful, fearing for the regime in himself, and must hold what we have said about poetry" (608a).

What separates the philosopher from the poet is the Socratic discovery of the question. The philosopher shares with the poet the importance of how meaning is put into language. For the poet, nothing can be wasted. Each and every syllable is given a necessary role; every level of a metaphor is present; every connection of words is precise and simple. The poem, when good, is always something beyond itself. It is never what it seems. This standard set by the poet must also be met by the philosopher.

Once the question enters into thought, nothing escapes the sphere of the question. The poet does not ask questions. Through the power of the metaphor the poet portrays, but does not question. The philosopher advances a metaphorical image in order to ask a question of it, or employs an analogy as a means for further posing the answer to a question. Once philosophy has command of the question, doubt enters into thought. Sceptical doubt, the attitude that drives philosophical thought, is not integral to poetry. Poetry is direct affirmation of the value and nature of the object. Philosophy can come to such affirmation only by passing through the process of doubt that engenders and is engendered by the formation of the question. Philosophical speech is not in principle able fully to enclose its object. The "what is," the *to ontos on,* always lies beyond what can be said of it in words. How the philosopher speaks makes all the difference in taking the mind as far as possible into the inner form of the real.

All poetry is a footnote to Homer as the poet of poets. All philosophy is a footnote to Plato as the philosopher of philosophers. Homer incorporates all that has gone before him in the myths of the Greek people. Plato incorporates all that has gone before him in the pronouncements of the pre-Socratics and the elenchus of Socrates. The ancient quarrel now is resolved. It bequeaths to us who come after it the dialectic between the image and the idea, between the metaphor as supplying the beginning points of thought and the question as supplying the continuance of thought.

7

Aristotle's Ethics

Diogenes Laertius says: "Aristotle [384–322 BC], son of Nicomachus and Phaestis, was a native of Stagira [in Macedonia]" (5.1). Nicomachus was of the medical guild of the Asclepiade (Asclepius, the hero and god of healing). At the age of seventeen he entered Plato's school at Athens, and he remained there until the death of Plato. Philip of Macedon invited him to act as tutor to Alexander. After the death of Philip, Aristotle returned to Athens and founded a school in a grove sacred to Apollo Lyceius and the Muses. An ancient tradition describes Aristotle as bald, thin-legged, with small eyes and a lisp in his speech, and as being noticeably well-dressed.

Aristotle's most widely read work is the *Nicomachean Ethics*, which stands in contrast to the modern ethical theories of both Immanuel Kant and John Stuart Mill. Kant, in *Groundwork of the Metaphysic of Morals*, says: "There is therefore only a single categorical imperative and it is this: '*Act only on that maxim through which you can at the same time will that it should become a universal law* [*Der kategorische Imperativ ist also nur ein einziger, und zwar dieser: handle nur nach derjenigen Maxime, durch die du zugleich wollen kannst, daß sie ein allgemeines Gesetz werde*].'"[24] Mill, in *Utilitarianism*, says: "The creed which accepts as the foundation of morals 'utility' or the 'greatest happiness principle' holds that actions are right in proportion as they tend to promote happiness; wrong as they tend to produce the reverse of happiness. By happiness is intended pleasure and the absence of pain; by unhappiness, pain and the privation of pleasure."[25]

---

24 Kant, *Groundwork*, 88.
25 Mill, *Utilitarianism*, 7.

Kant's "categorical imperative" and Mill's "greatest happiness principle" portray ethics as requiring a decision procedure through which an individual faced with a moral situation can decide right from wrong. But neither Kant's principle nor Mill's principle will provide human action with what course to take in a particular situation. The most that can be claimed is Mill's observation that: "Though the application of the standard may be difficult, it is better than none at all."[26] Kant places the individual in a perpetual state of fault or guilt (*Schuld*) because it is impossible to know if one has successfully fulfilled the standard of the categorical imperative. The approach to ethics of both Kant and Mill is that moral judgment depends upon an analysis of the factors involved in any given situation; there is no need to have a metaphysical comprehension of the good as the ultimate principle at which all human action properly aims or to cultivate character as the basis of moral action. To aim at the good and the development of good character may be desirable, but they are not the essence of ethics. Kant and Mill approach ethics as if it were a form of scientific reasoning. Aristotle conceives ethics as an art.

Aristotle, in *Nicomachean Ethics*, understands morality as based in character (*ēthos*). Character is acquired through habit—by repeatedly acting in accord with virtue, we become virtuous. The human being that possesses the intellectual virtue of prudence (*phronēsis*) is able to pursue the correct action in a given circumstance and to do so by acting in accordance with correct reason (*orthos logos*). Ethics is not simply concerned with how to choose right from wrong in a given problematic situation. Ethics is concerned with how to choose the best life. Aristotle says, in the first sentence of his work, that: "Every art [*technē*] and every inquiry, and similarly every action as well as choice is held to aim at some good" (1094a). The good at which human beings aim is *eudaimonia*, which is, literally, the condition of having a good daimon, or genius. To be a success as a person, the person needs

---

26   Ibid., 26.

to be endowed with a good spirit. Good-spiritedness is innate to such a person.

Aristotle says: "We posit the work of a human being as a certain life, and this is an activity of soul and actions accompanied by reason, the work of a serious human being to do these things well and nobly, and each thing is brought to completion well in accord with the virtue proper to it—if this is so, then the human good becomes an activity of soul in accord with virtue, and if there are several virtues, then in accord with the best and most complete one" (1098a). What human beings desire most in life is happiness in the sense of knowing how to act well and in accordance with the good. In any particular instance the good is present in the form of a virtue. A virtue is that good that is appropriate to the action taken. Virtue (*aretē*) is the excellence of a specific type of thing that marks the peak of that thing and allows for what is done to be done well. A particular situation may require the virtue of courage (*andreia*), or it may require moderation (*sōphrosunē*), or liberality (*eleutheriotēs*), or the most important virtue of all—justice (*dikaiosunē*). These and the other virtues are guides to achieving the good in relation to a particular action. We are happy when we apprehend ourselves as being successful at being a human being.

Virtuous actions are first instilled in us as children, as habits, by adults who are virtuous. Later we deliberately attempt to accomplish virtuous actions as the basis of our desire to become proper and full human beings. Only human beings engage in moral choice. Acting in accord with virtue is an art. As with any art, practicing the art time after time is essential for its acquisition. Aristotle says: "Whatever deeds arise in accord with the virtues are not done justly or moderately if they are merely in a certain state, but only if he who does those deeds is in a certain state as well: first, if he acts knowingly; second, if he acts by choosing and by choosing the actions in question for their own sake; and third, if he acts while being in a steady and unwavering state" (1105a). As mentioned above, choice also requires "acting in accord with correct reason" (1103b). Correct reason is the means for finding the middle term (*to meson*) or the mean (*hē mesotēs*).

Aristotle says: "Virtue, therefore, is a characteristic marked by choice, residing in the mean relative to us, a characteristic defined by reason and as the prudent person would define it. Virtue is also a mean with respect to two vices, the one vice related to excess, the other to deficiency; and further it is a mean because some vices fall short of and others exceed what should be the case in both passions and actions, whereas virtue discovers and chooses the middle term" (1107a). Courage (*andreia*), for example, is a mean between the vice of excessive fearlessness or recklessness (*thrasutēs*) and the vice of cowardice (*deilia*), ignoble timidity in a need for action or lack of resolution in the face of the hostility of sentiments held by others. Liberality (*eleutheriotēs*) is the mean between the vices of prodigality (*asōtia*) and stinginess (*aneleutheria*).

As mentioned above, Aristotle's ethics is concerned not only with how to achieve the good through virtues as governing our actions, but also with the choice of the best life. Aristotle says: "The especially prominent ways of life are three: the one just mentioned [the pursuit of pleasure], the political [the pursuit of power and awards], and, the third, the contemplative" (1095b). Aristotle regards the life devoted to money-making as not properly an end in itself. Money is a means to an end, such as securing pleasure or political power. Aristotle holds that the best life is that devoted to contemplation (*theōria*). He says: "So for a human being, this is the life that accords with the intellect, if in fact this especially *is* a human being. This life, therefore, is also the happiest" (1178a). To be human is to be able to use the intellect to contemplate. In order to contemplate, leisure is required, as well as prudence or practical wisdom. Leisure and prudence place us in the position by which thought can be cultivated for its own sake.

Contemplation is a self-sufficient activity in that it does not aim at an end that is more than itself. It is a divine activity. Aristotle says: "That complete happiness is a certain contemplative activity would appear also from this: we have supposed that the gods especially are blessed and happy. . . . . the activity of the god, because it is superior in blessedness, would be contemplative. And so in the case of the human activities, the one that is most akin to this would be most characterized by happiness. A sign of this is also that the rest of the animals do not share in happiness, because they are completely deprived of such an activity." Human beings stand between the animals and gods. "For to the gods, life as a whole is blessed; but to human beings, it is blessed to the extent that something resembling such an activity is available. But none of the other animals are happy, since they in no way share in contemplation. Happiness, then, is also coextensive with contemplation" (1178b).

Aristotle's description of the contemplative life is a description of the life dominated by the philosophic spirit. Aristotle says: "The person who is active in accord with the intellect, who cares for this and is in the best condition regarding it, also seems to be dearest to the gods. . . . And that all these things are available to the wise person especially is not unclear. He is the dearest to the gods, therefore, and it is likely that this same person is also happiest. As a result, in this way too, the wise person would be especially happy" (1179a). The genius that must inhabit the human being to provide *eudaimonia* is present in those who engage in the love of wisdom. For happiness, more is required than a decision procedure to judge right from wrong actions. Once character is secured such judgment comes naturally, the ability to choose correctly having been acquired by the experience gained from the habit of consistently acting in accordance with virtue.

8

Lucretius's Poem

Titus Lucretius Carus (probably 94 to 55 BC) was likely a member of the aristocratic Roman family of the Lucretii. There is also a theory, but not fully supported, that Lucretius was a landowner near Pompeii and acquired his knowledge of Epicureanism at Naples. The only fact that is certain about his life is that he was a friend of Memmins, the aristocrat to whom his poem is dedicated. The title of the poem, *De rerum natura* (*On the Nature of Things*) is a Latin translation of the Greek title of Epicurus's chief work, *On Nature* [*Physis*], as well as that of Empedocles's poem, *On Nature*. Lucretius greatly admired Empedocles. In the invocation to his book-length poem, Lucretius portrays the figure of Venus (the Empedoclean principle of Love) as opposite Mars (the Empedoclean principle of Strife). The purpose of *De rerum natura* is to present the essential elements of Epicurus's philosophy and, in so doing, to relieve us of the fear of death.

The naturalistic philosopher George Santayana, in *Three Philosophical Poets: Lucretius, Dante, Goethe*, says: "Since Lucretius is thus identified for us with his poem, and is lost in his philosophy, the antecedents of Lucretius are simply stages by which his conception of nature first shaped itself in the human mind.... A naturalistic conception of things is a great work of the imagination,—greater, I think, than any dramatic or moral mythology: it is a conception fit to inspire great poetry, and in the end, perhaps, it will prove the only conception able to inspire it."[27] Santayana says, further: "Naturalism is a philosophy of observation, and of an imagination that extends the observable; all the sights and sounds enter into it, and lend it their directness, pungency, and coercive stress..... The naturalistic poet abandons

---

27 Santayana, 14–15.

fairy land, because he has discovered nature, history, the actual passions of man."[28] Lucretius is using poetry as a way to impress what Epicurus has said on present and future generations.

In one of his letters to his brother Quintus, Cicero says: "Lucretius's poetry is as you say—sparking with natural genius, but plenty of technical skill" (14.3). Although Cicero does not agree with the philosophy of Epicureanism, he nonetheless admires the genius of Lucretius as a poet. Lucretius says: "For I shall begin to discourse to you upon the most high system of heaven and of the gods, and I shall disclose the first-beginnings of things [atoms], from which nature makes all things and increases and nourishes them, and into which the same nature again reduces them when dissolved" (1.54-57). In so doing, Lucretius says he will free us from "superstition, which displayed her head from the regions of heaven, lowering over mortals with horrible aspect, a man of Greece [Epicurus] was the first that dared to uplift mortal eyes against her, the first to make a stand against her" (1.63-67). The philosophy of Epicurus can offer us an understanding of natural events without resorting to fables of the gods. For Epicurus, as well as for Lucretius, the gods exist within the order of nature. The gods do not govern what occurs in nature.

Once we truly grasp the order of things, as Epicurus teaches, we will realize that what is, is not the result of a single substance that underlies the many things of the world as its consequents. We will also realize that what is, is not the result of the four elements—earth, air, fire, and water—mixing together to form the things of the world. We will see that all that there is, is the product of atoms falling through the void and swerving and coming together in an indefinite number of ways, such that they form the things of the world, including ourselves. How the atoms combine is due to chance. Lucretius says: "For certainly neither did the first-beginnings place themselves by design each in its own order with keen intelligence, nor assuredly did they make agreement what motions each should produce; but because, being many and

---

28   Ibid., 24-25.

shifted in many ways, they are harried and set in motion with blows throughout the universe from infinity, thus by trying every kind of motion and combination, at length they fall into such arrangements as this sum of things consists of" (1.1021–128; cf. 5.187–94 and 422–31).

Things come into being and dissolve and pass out of being by chance. Human beings are no exception. Human beings are composed of mind and body. Lucretius says: "The mind [*mens*] is begotten along with the body [*corpus*], and grows up with it, and with it grows old. . . . It follows therefore that the whole nature of the spirit [*animus*] is dissolved abroad, like smoke, into high winds of air, since we can see it begotten along with the body, and growing up with it, and as I have shown, falling to pieces at the same time worn out with age" (3.445–58). The spirit or soul is not immortal. It is only different from the body because it is "composed of minute particles and elements much smaller than the flowing liquid of water or cloud or smoke" (3.426–28). When we accept the mortality of the immaterial along with the material, the soul with the body, we are relieved of the fear of death.

We can turn to the words of Epicurus as quoted by Diogenes Laertius: "Accustom thyself to believe that death is nothing to us, for good and evil imply sentience, and death is the privation of all sentience. . . . For life has no terrors for him who has thoroughly apprehended that there are no terrors for him in ceasing to live. . . . Death, therefore, the most awful of evils is nothing to us, seeing that, when we are, death is not come, and when death is come, we are not" (10.125).

The famous garden of Epicurus is the response to this elimination of the fear of death. We may withdraw from the ups and downs, the back and forth, of society and seek to enjoy life's pleasures, the greatest pleasure of which is peace of mind (*ataraxia*). According to Diogenes Laertius, Epicurus claims: "He who has a clear and certain understanding of these things will direct every preference and aversion toward securing health of body and tranquility of mind, seeing that this is the sum and end of a blessed life. For the end of all our actions is to be free from pain and fear, and, when once we have attained all this, the tempest of the soul is laid" (D.L.10.128).

In the fifth book of *De rerum natura*, Lucretius attaches to his account of the natural world an account of the human world, in which he gives an extensive description of how society develops, from the crudest conditions of human existence to the acquisition of language, the discovery of metals, the beginnings of cultivation, and the formation of the arts. Lucretius says: "When they had got themselves huts and skins and fire, and woman mated with man moved into one [home, and the laws of wedlock] became known, and they saw offspring born of them, then the first human race began to grow soft" (5.1011–14). Human beings learned that they could provide for themselves in terms of their ingenuity. Lucretius concludes the fifth book with the observation: "So by degrees time brings up before us every single thing, and reason lifts it into the precincts of light. For they saw one thing after another grow clear in their minds, until they attained the highest pinnacle of the arts" (5.1454–57).

Lucretius also warns that all of this human development takes place within the natural world and is subject to the events of nature, such as earthquakes and plagues. Moreover, the world itself is mortal. Lucretius says: "In the first place, since the earth's mass and the water, the wind's light breezes, and burning heat, which are seen to compose this sum of things, all consist of a body that is born and dies, we must consider the whole world to be of the same structure. . . . Therefore, when I see the grand parts and members of the world being consumed and born again, I may be sure that heaven and earth also once had their time of beginning and will have their destruction" (5.235–46).

Lucretius has transposed the philosophy of Epicurus into an epic poem for the Latin reader. He has shown how all of physical nature can be comprehended by a metaphysics of material causes and how human society develops within it as an extension of human nature, with the warning that society does not overcome the forces of nature that surround it. All is mortal, including the human soul. Knowing this fact about ourselves, we can accept our own mortality, because we cannot alter it. It is the constant condition of life. Once we accept this condition we may seek to enjoy our existence as human as much as we can, while we can.

Part Three
Christians

9

Boethius's Consolation

Anicius Maulius Severinus Boethius (c. 480–c. 524) was of high birth, the son of a consul (the supreme civil and military magistrate of Rome, under the Republic), who became consul himself in 510. He was educated in Athens, where he acquired a knowledge of the various schools of Greek philosophy, on the basis of which he set himself the task of translating the complete works of Plato and Aristotle into Latin and, in so doing, to show the agreement of their philosophical principles. Although he did not complete this project, he did translate the whole of Aristotle's *Organon* (Aristotle's logic) as well as Porphyry's introduction, the *Isagoge*. He also commented at length on Aristotle's *Categories* and *On Interpretation*. He wrote several theological tractates, including *The Trinity is One God not Three Gods* and *On the Catholic Faith*.

Boethius was accused of treason and imprisoned at Pavia, in Lombardy, northern Italy, near Milan, and brutally put to death in 524. While in prison he wrote the *Philosophiae consolationis, The Consolation of Philosophy*. This became a work of universal appeal throughout the Middle Ages. It was translated into Anglo-Saxon, German, and French, and its readership included Dante, Boccaccio, and Chaucer. The term *consolatio* is the source for the English word "consolation," meaning comfort or solace, the meaning that it carries in classical Latin. In Late Latin (as used by the early Church fathers and by other writers, beginning in the third century) *consolatio* has the meaning of help, support.[29] Notable is a lost treatise of Cicero, titled *De Consolatione*, which he cites in *Tusculan Disputations* (3.31.76) in the context of the need to

---

29 Cf. the entries for *consolatio* in Lewis and Short, *Latin Dictionary*, 434, and Niermeyer and van de Kieft, *Lexicon*, 1:336.

speak so as to do away with distress in the mind of someone mourning a loss.

It seems likely that Boethius intends the title of his work to endorse the value of philosophy, both in the sense of providing comfort and relief of distress and in the sense of support by bringing reason into connection with faith, combining both senses of *consolatio*. Christianity comes into the world as a revealed religion, as a doctrine, delivered by Christ, of redemption, salvation, and divine love. As revealed religion, it is not a theoretical system. The truth of Christian doctrine as revealed is a matter of faith. But in understanding this doctrine, faith may be joined with reason. Boethius's *Consolation of Philosophy* is a *prosimetrum*, prose interspersed with verse.[30] This style of expression allows Boethius to join faith with reason. His verses affect the passions and direct the reader toward faith. His prose narratives take the reader into lines of reasoning that support his claims. His alteration of verse and prose provides the reader with an agreeable dialectic of faith (*fides*) and reason (*ratio*), the two factors that came to dominate the thought of the Middle Ages. Boethius is the last of the Roman philosophers, taking philosophy from the Greeks, and the first of the Scholastic theologians, applying reason to faith.

The first pages of Boethius's *Consolation* are among the best presentations of the philosophic spirit in the history of philosophy. His work opens with a poem describing how easily fortune (*fortuna*) can change from positive to negative. He finds himself as "one now fallen" (1.1.22). In the prose passage that follows, Boethius says: "While I was thinking these thoughts to myself in silence, and set my pen to record this tearful complaint, there seemed to stand above my head a woman. Her look filled me with awe.... Her dress was made of very fine, imperishable thread, of delicate workmanship.... On its lower border was woven the Greek Π letter (P), and on the upper, Θ (Th) [for

---

30 For a definitive account of this feature of Boethius's work, see Blackwood, *"Consolation" of Boethius.*

practical philosophy and theoretical philosophy], and between the two letters steps were marked like a ladder, by which one might climb from the lower letter to the higher" (1.1.1–22).

His visitor proceeds to act on his behalf. Boethius says: "Now when she saw the Muses of poetry standing by my bed, helping me to find words for my grief, she was disturbed for a moment, and then cried out with fiercely blazing eyes: 'Who let these theatrical tarts in with this sick man? Not only have they no cures for his pain, but with their sweet poison they make it worse.'" These were the Helicon Muses of which Hesiod speaks, who can sing both true and false songs. The visitor continues: "'Get out, you Sirens, beguiling men straight to their destruction! Leave him to *my* Muses to care for and restore to health.' Thus upbraided, that company of the Muses dejectedly hung their heads, confessing their shame by their blushes, and dismally left my room" (1.1.26–44). The visitor then speaks in verse, describing Boethius's pitiable condition and how he has fallen from what he once was.

The visitor asks: "Do you recognize me? . . . He will soon recover—he did, after all, know me before" (1.2.7–13). Boethius says: "So, when I looked on her clearly and steadily, I saw the nurse who brought me up, whose house I had from my youth frequented, the lady Philosophy [*Philosophia*]." Boethius asks her why she has come. Lady Philosophy replies: "It could not be right that Philosophy should leave an innocent man companionless on the road. . . . Do you think that this is the first time that Wisdom [*sapientia*] has been attacked and endangered by a wicked society?" (1.3.3–17). Lady Philosophy then speaks at length of the death of Socrates, of Anaxagoras's flight from Athens, and of Zeno's sufferings. Indeed, those who practice philosophy and the philosopher's way of life can expect conflict with much of society.

Boethius proceeds, at great length and in much detail, to put forth the meaning of Christian doctrine in neo-Platonic philosophical terms. He then comes to his conclusion: "There remains also an observer from on high fore-knowing all things, God, and the always present eternity of his sight runs along with the future quality of our actions dispensing rewards for the good and punishment for the wicked. . . . Turn away then from vices, cultivate virtues, lift up your mind to righteous hopes, offer up humble prayers to heaven. A great necessity is solemnly ordained for you if you do not want to deceive yourselves, to do good when you act before the eyes of a judge who sees all things" (5.6.166–76). Boethius affirms the doctrine that God is omnipresent and omniscient. His consolation is complete. He has not simply invoked faith to justify his claims; he has shown that his claims are supported by philosophical reason.

Vico calls Boethius "Latino Platone"[31] and "il Platon Cristiano."[32] Boethius's spirit is that of Christianized humanism. He writes about himself and the condition in which he finds himself, but he does so in a manner such that his particular condition, under a pending sentence of death, is part of the human condition itself. He has a sense of stoicism, found in every philosopher—even the Epicurean—that, wherever the philosopher is, the philosopher seeks a form of wisdom that will allow for an acceptance of what is. But what is, for the philosopher, includes the ideal and the unseen that is within the seen, the intelligible in the perceptible. Boethius, in his *prosimetrum*, not only joins the emotions grounded in faith with the coherence of reason, he demonstrates the connection of the imagination with ratiocination. He presents himself as a master image, a *topos*, from which he brings forth the speech of both reason and faith, containing the ideas and the passions that form the human being. It is his style of thought that accounts for why his *Consolation* has commanded such attention for those seeking to gain insight into the essence of philosophy and its relation to faith over so many centuries.

---

31 Vico, *Institutiones*, 246.
32 Vico, *Epistole*, 167.

10

Anselm's Argument

St. Anselm (1033-1109) was born of a noble family in Aosta, in Piedmont, northern Italy. He entered the Benedictine order in 1060, at the Abbey of Bec in Normandy. He became Prior of Bec in 1063 and Abbot in 1078. In 1093 he became Archbishop of Canterbury and Primate of England. Anselm's most famous achievement is his ontological argument for the existence of God. The major modern interpreter and supporter of Anselm's argument, Charles Hartshorne, rightly says: "There is no more famous philosophical argument than his [Anselm's] so-called 'ontological' proof for God's existence."[33] Anyone who undertakes the study of philosophy encounters this argument early on and eventually must take a stand on its interpretation and validity. Anselm states his argument in his work, *Proslogium or Discourse on the Existence of God*.

Anselm conceives his "discourse" as an allocution, that is, as an authoritative or hortatory address. His purpose is to determine whether there might be a single argument that would verify the belief he holds in the existence of God. As he puts it: "I began to ask myself whether there might be found a single argument which would require no other for its proof than itself alone."[34] He is correct in this aim, for, in logic, if more than one argument is advanced for a single conclusion, either the further argument is redundant or the original argument is defective. Adding arguments together to prove a point means either the point is unprovable or its possible proof is not fully known.

Anselm says: "Therefore, if that, than which nothing greater can be conceived, exists in the understanding alone, the very being, than which nothing greater can be conceived, is one, than which a greater can be conceived. But obviously this is impossible. Hence, there is no doubt that there exists a being, than which

---

33   Hartshorne, "Introduction," 1.
34   Anselm, *Writings*, 1.

nothing greater can be conceived, and it exists both in the understanding and in reality."[35] Anselm's claim is that in *one and only one case* the thought of something necessarily entails its existence—the case of the thought of a being of which nothing greater exists. The essence of the argument can be stated in terms of two premisses and a conclusion:

> I can conceive in my understanding of a being greater than which none other exists.
> This being must exist in reality independent of my conception of it, or it would not be the greatest such being.
> Therefore, God exists both in my understanding and in reality.

In Ecclesiastes is: "God is in heaven and you upon earth; therefore let your words be few" (5:2). Anselm's words are few and precise. His intention in the argument is to demonstrate that any attempt to deny the existence of God is a contradiction. His opponent is the fool who has said in his heart that there is no God (Psalms 14:1). The fool has said this in his heart, but, as the argument demonstrates, the fool cannot do so in the fool's understanding. Appended to Anselm's work is a brief text, "In Behalf of the Fool: An Answer to the Argument of Anselm in the Proslogium, by Gaunilon, a Monk of Marmoutier." Gaunilon says: "But of God, or a being greater than all others, I could not conceive at all, except merely according to the word. And an object can hardly or never be conceived according to the word alone."[36] Gaunilon's claim is that there is no necessity that anyone must have such a conception in the understanding. God may simply be a word, not a concept. If God is simply a word there is no argument because argument is always conceptual.

Gaunilon further raises the example of a perfect island. If we conceive of such a perfect entity, does that entail that it exists? We may conceive of a perfect entity and also deny its existence in reality, but in so doing we are not involved in a self-contradiction. Gaunilon says: "You can no longer doubt that this island which is more excellent than all lands exists somewhere, since you have no doubt that it is in your understanding."[37] Anselm replies to this

---

35   Ibid, 8.
36   Ibid., 148–49.
37   Ibid., 151.

example by reminding Gaunilon that: "The non-existence, then, of that than which a greater cannot be conceived is inconceivable."[38] Only if the perfection of the island was conceived as more perfect than any conceivable perfection would it be a self-contradiction to deny it. Anselm is not claiming that the thought of something perfect entails its existence. We often think of what would be an ideal state of affairs, but we do not claim it exists or must exist.

Anselm's argument for the existence of God demonstrates that the thought of a being greater than which none other exists necessarily entails the thought of its existence. The circle of thought is never left. In every other instance, the thought of an object can be regarded as distinct from the thought of the existence of the object as well as from the actual existence of the object. Anselm's argument, in both logical and rhetorical terms, shows what it means, in metaphysics, to have thought think itself. God's existence is pure thought. Gaunilon and all the critics since have missed that *thought exists*. Anselm's argument proves that if thought itself exists, it can verify the existence of the absolute form of itself. The rational is the real.

In his *Monologium*, that accompanies his *Proslogium*, Anselm says he engages in a soliloquy. His soliloquy is not a scholastic argument, as is the purpose of the *Proslogium*. It is a meditation on the being of God, with the intention that: "Nothing in Scripture should be urged on the authority of Scripture itself, but that whatever the conclusion of independent investigation should declare to be true, should in an unadorned style, with common proofs and with a simple argument, be briefly enforced by the cogency of reason, and plainly expounded in the light of truth."[39] Anselm's aim is to combine faith, based on Scripture, with reason.

In his *Monologium*, Anselm is concerned to discover how the various attributes of God are connected to God's existence. The primary concern of human beings is to determine what is good. Anselm says: "It is natural that this man should, at some time, turn his mind's eye to the examination of that cause by which these things are good, which he does not desire, except as he

---

38 Ibid., 159.
39 Ibid., 35.

judges them to be good."[40] Anselm's reasoning is Neoplatonic in that good is described as a form that exists as such, not through anything else, and provides the absolute standard by means of which something is said to be good in comparison with another.

Anselm says, of those things that are good: "Who can doubt this very being, through which all goods exist, to be a great good? This must be, then, a good through itself, since every other good is through it."[41] God is the cause of all that exists and whatever exists as a good is the result of God's goodness. In his conclusion to the *Monologium*, Anselm says: "It is established that through the supreme Good and its supremely wise omnipotence all things were created and live."[42] Anselm's purpose is to prove the existence of God by his unique argument and also to show that as the greatest being God has the greatest attributes. The greatest attribute of all is Goodness. Divine goodness is the absolute standard against which human goodness can be measured. Divine goodness makes ethics possible.

Why is Anselm's argument for God's existence unique? The answer can be found in Hegel's assessment, at the end of his section on Anselm, in his *Lectures on the History of Philosophy*.[43] Hegel says that in Anselm's argument self-consciousness secures for the first time a grasp of the beyond (*Jenseits*) within the finitude of human existence. It is a first glimpse of what Hegel, in his *Science of Logic*, calls the "true infinite" (*das wahrhafte Unendliche*) — the sense in which consciousness sees the infinite, not as a simple beyond but as a process in which consciousness is self-determining — always fashioning itself into new shapes or moments that both cancel yet transcend what has gone before. Anselm's argument allows us to understand ourselves as finite beings, always attempting to transcend our finitude.

---

40   Ibid., 38.
41   Ibid., 40.
42   Ibid., 143–44.
43   Hegel, *Vorlesungen*, 560.

11

Cusanus's Learned Ignorance

Nicholas of Cusa (Nicholas Cusanus) (1401-1464) was born at Kues, between Trier and Koblenz, on the Moselle River in Germany. He studied philosophy at Heidelberg, canon law at Padua, and theology at Cologne. He became a priest between 1436 and 1440. He served as a member of a papal commission sent to Constantinople to negotiate with the Greek Church for plans to enact a reunion with Rome. He was made a Cardinal in 1448 and Bishop of Brixen in 1450. He had a lifelong interest in collecting classical and medieval manuscripts, and made the notable discovery of twelve lost comedies of the Latin playwright Plautus. Cusanus's most famous work is *De Docta Ignorantia – On Learned Ignorance* (1440).

Cusanus's conception of learned ignorance is an extension of Socratic ignorance. Cusanus says: "We desire to know that we do not know. If we can fully attain unto this [knowledge of our ignorance] we will attain unto learned ignorance. For a man— even one very well versed in learning—will attain unto nothing more perfect than to be found to be most learned in the ignorance which is distinctively his. The more he knows that he is unknowing, the more learned he will be. Unto this end I have undertaken the task of writing a few things about learned ignorance."[44] Cusanus begins modern philosophy with a doctrine of ignorance as Socrates begins ancient philosophy with his doctrine of ignorance—his claim to know only that he does not know.

Ernst Cassirer, in his study of the Renaissance, says that Cusanus can be characterized as "the first modern thinker" because he approaches the question of God in terms of "the possibility of knowledge about God,"[45] which is a departure from the traditional approach of speculative theology. Cusanus equates

---

44 Nicholas of Cusa, *Learned Ignorance*, 50–51.
45 Cassirer, *Individual and the Cosmos*, 10.

God with the conception of the Absolute Maximum. He defines this conception in Anselmian terms: "Now, I give the name 'Maximum' to that than which there cannot be anything greater. . . . Thus, the Maximum is the Absolute One which is all things. And all things are in the Maximum (for it is the Maximum); and since nothing is opposed to it, the Minimum likewise coincides with it, and hence the Maximum is also in all things."[46] Cassirer regards Cusanus as having introduced the modern sense of the problem of knowledge that is reinforced by Cusanus's use of mathematics to demonstrate the coincidence of absolute Maximum and absolute Minimum. Cusanus says: "For *maximum* is a superlative just as *minimum* is a superlative. Therefore, it is not the case that absolute quantity is maximum quantity rather than minimum quantity; for in it the minimum is the maximum coincidingly."[47]

The finite intellect cannot really attain to the truth of things because it can know only what something is in terms of its opposites, its likeness or unlikeness to something else. Cusanus says: "Hence, the intellect, which is not truth, never comprehends truth so precisely that truth cannot be comprehended infinitely more precisely. For the intellect is to truth as [an inscribed] polygon is to [the inscribing] circle. The more angles the inscribed polygon has the more similar it is to the circle. However, even if the number of its angles is increased *ad infinitum*, the polygon never becomes equal [to the circle] unless it is resolved into an identity with the circle."[48] We can never possess what anything is in its own being, what it is in and of itself (its quiddity). Cusanus says: "Therefore, the quiddity of things, which is the truth of beings, is unattainable in its purity; though it is sought by all philosophers, it is found by no one as it is. And the more deeply we are instructed in this ignorance, the closer we approach to truth."[49]

Cusanus insists that God is not a name, because: "Anything than which a greater or lesser cannot be posited cannot be named.

---

46 Nicholas of Cusa, *Learned Ignorance*, 51.
47 Ibid., 53.
48 Ibid., 52.
49 Ibid., 53.

For by the movement of our reason names are assigned to things which, in terms of comparative relation, can be comparatively greater or lesser."[50] As the absolute Maximum, God is not greater or lesser in divine being. That God is not a name can be illustrated by the scale of numbers. In such a scale we can progress toward the idea of a maximum number, but we can never come to it because there is always possible a greater number. We can see that: "Oneness is the beginning of all number, because it is the minimum; and it is the end of all number, because it is the maximum."[51] Thus "Absolute oneness" is the proper designation for the "unnameable God" and God is everything that is possible. Absolute oneness can never be greater or lesser.

Cusanus, from the perspective of his concept of the Maximum, gives a version of the ontological argument for God's existence. He says: "How, then—since minimally being is maximally being—could we rightly think that the Maximum is able not to exist? Moreover, we cannot rightly think that something exists in the absence of being. But Absolute Being cannot be other than the absolutely Maximum. Hence, we cannot rightly think that something exists in the absence of the [absolutely] Maximum."[52]

Cusanus's master image of the Maximum is the infinite line. He says: "I maintain, therefore, that if there were an infinite line, it would be a straight line, a triangle, a circle, and a sphere. And likewise if there were an infinite sphere, it would be a circle, a triangle, and a line. And the same thing must be said about an infinite triangle and an infinite circle."[53] An infinite line exists only in thought. Cusanus is asking us to engage in a thought-experiment to verify his conception of the coincidence of maximum and minimum. He provides a drawing of a vertical line with several curved lines touching it at the center point of their curvature. We can easily imagine that as the curvature of these lines would expand, they would flatten out so as to approach a

---

50 Ibid., 54.
51 Ibid., 55.
52 Ibid., 56.
53 Ibid., 63.

straight line until there would be an absolute minimum distance between the expansion of their curvature and the straight line.

Cusanus puts this point as follows: "First of all, it is evident that an infinite line would be a straight line. The diameter of a circle is a straight line, and the circumference is a curved line which is greater than the diameter. So if the curved line becomes less curved in proportion to the increased circumference of the circle, then the circumference of the maximum circle, which cannot be greater, is minimally curved and therefore maximally straight. Hence, the minimum coincides with the maximum — to such an extent that we can visually recognize that it is necessary for the maximum line to be maximally straight and minimally curved."[54]

What is our learned ignorance, now that we have before us Cusanus's thought-experiment? We are able to visualize how the infinite is within the finite and the finite in the infinite, without reducing one to the other. Yet we cannot say more than this. Whatever knowledge the intellect develops about the world will have this coincidence within it, but it will offer us only a partial truth, because each instance of knowledge will contain the possibility of being surpassed by a greater attainment of knowledge.

Yet this progression of what is known is itself a whole that already is, but is not fully known. Our ignorance of the whole as the whole must be accepted. Once accepted, it leaves us free to pursue the problem of knowledge in every way possible, without the illusion that we can have perfect knowledge within our finitude. Cusanus has made way for the modern conception of knowledge to emerge from medieval theology, without opposing the principles that remain with that theology. He has also made possible the pursuit of a self-determining metaphysics that frees philosophy from its role of servant to theology. Once the philosopher is allowed to claim ignorance, contemplation becomes a self-determining process.

---

54 Ibid.

12

Bruno's Infinite Worlds

Giordano Bruno (1548–1600) was born at Nola, near Naples. At an early age he entered the Dominican order. In 1576 he was accused of heresy. He fled the Dominican order and began his wanderings through Europe, which caused him to take up residence in Switzerland, England, France, and Germany, specifically including London and Oxford, Paris, Wittenberg, and Frankfurt. He signed his many publications "Giordano Bruno, the Nolan" (Giordano Bruno Nolando). "The Nolan" occupied the place, on the title pages of his writings, where he would have identified himself as a Dominican, had he remained in the order. In August 1591, Bruno returned to Italy at the invitation of a Venetian nobleman. He was arrested by the Inquisition and taken to prison. At his trial he recanted the heresies with which he was charged, but he was sent to Rome for a further trial. He remained in prison at Rome for eight years, at the end of which he was sentenced as a heretic, having this time refused to recant. He was burned alive on Thursday, February 16, 1600, in the Campo de' Fiori. His tongue was fixed shut, because of the fear the authorities had of his power of speech.

Bruno is the most famous among the Italian philosophers of the Renaissance. He is the author of a wide range of highly original works on metaphysics and ethics. An exceptional work on Bruno's thought is Frances Yates, *Giordano Bruno and the Hermetic Tradition*. Yates says: "The great forward movements of the Renaissance all derive their vigour, their emotional impulse, from looking backwards."[55] Bruno holds that Christ was a magus (from Greek *magos*), a person with supernatural powers, and that the magical religion of the Egyptians was better than Christianity. Prominent in Egyptian thought is Hermes Trismegistus (Thrice-great Hermes); or "Thoth the very great." His greatness is emphasized by the trifold repetition. The Hermetic philosophy is

---

55 Yates, *Bruno*, 1.

based on the art of memory, though which the original meanings of words and images are brought forth. Bruno apparently believed that the religious and moral doctrines he embraced could be resolved within a Catholic framework.

I wish to consider only one part of Bruno's very complicated writings, his *On the Infinite Universe and Worlds* (*De L'infinito Universo et Mondi*), especially its "Fifth Dialogue." It is influenced by Lucretius's *De rerum natura*. Bruno's cosmology takes us in a further direction from what is said concerning the sense of the ultimate put forth by Anselm and Cusanus.

In his "Introductory Epistle" to this work, Bruno quotes Lucretius's discussion of the infinite: "Besides, if all the existing space be granted for the moment to be finite, suppose someone proceeded to the very extremest edge and cast a flying lance, do you prefer that the lance forcibly thrown goes whither it was sent and flies afar, or do you think that anything can hinder and obstruct it? . . . For whether there is something to hinder and keep it from going whither it is sent and from fixing itself at its mark, or whether it passes out, that was no boundary whence it was sped" (*De rerum natura*, 1.968–73; 977–79).[56] If the lance goes on, then there is space beyond. If the lance does not go on, then it encounters matter. In either event, it is not the end of the universe. We cannot imagine space as finite. If it were finite, we could go to its boundary. Once at the boundary, what is beyond the boundary is more space, and so on, *ad infinitum*.

In *Cause, Principle and Unity*, Bruno considers Cusanus's conception of the coincidence of the Maximum and Minimum. Bruno says: "He who wants to know the greatest secrets of nature should observe and examine the minima and maxima of contraries and opposites. There is a profound magic in knowing how to extract the contrary from the contrary, after having discovered their point of union."[57] This magic is dependent on the insight that the finite is possible only as the contrary of the infinite. The finite is a boundary within the infinite.

In the fifth dialogue of *On the Infinite Universe and Worlds*, Philotheo, speaking for Bruno, says that when you have

---

56   Bruno, *Infinite*, 231.
57   Bruno, *Cause*, 100.

understood that the finite and infinite are a coincidence of opposites, "you will no longer say that there is an edge or limit either to the extent or to the motion of the universe; you will esteem the belief in a *primum mobile*, an uppermost and all-containing heaven, to be a vain fantasy. You will conceive rather a general womb in which are situate all worlds alike, even as this terrestrial globe in this our local space is surrounded by our atmosphere and is in no way nailed or attached to any other body, nor hath any base but its own centre."[58] The *primum mobile* is literally the first moving thing. It is the outermost concentric sphere in the medieval version of Ptolemaic astronomy, in which are the fixed stars and the planets in its daily rotation. Bruno is arguing against the claim, in Aristotelianism, that the *primum mobile* is the highest physical sphere that has its circular motion directly from God as the unmoved mover.

Philotheo says: "It is then unnecessary to investigate whether there be beyond the heaven Space, Void or Time. For there is a single general space, a single vast immensity which we may freely call void; in it are innumerable (*innumerabili et infiniti*) globes like this one on which we live and grow. This space we believe to be infinite, since neither reason, convenience, possibility, sense-perception or nature assign to it a limit. In it are an infinity of worlds (*infiniti mondi*) similar to our own, and of the same kind."[59] The universe is not limited to our world or simply surrounding only our world. It is the spatial and temporal receptacle of an indefinite number of complete worlds.

Bruno's presentation of his cosmology continues. Each of these worlds is a living being. "For each world in the ethereal field occupieth his own space, so that one toucheth not nor thrusteth against the other; but they pursue their courses and are situate at such a distance that contraries destroy not but rather comfort one another." These worlds are not necessary for the perfection and subsistence of our own world, "but that for the subsistence and perfection of the universe itself an infinity of worlds is indeed necessary."[60] Bruno makes it clear that this view of the cosmos

---

58 Bruno, *Infinite*, 361.
59 Ibid., 363.
60 Ibid., 376.

must be maintained against the voice of the multitude, against the view that our world is the center of the universe and is unique.

Our world is rightly understood as simply one among many. He says: "Break and hurl to earth with the resounding whirlwind of lively reasoning those fantasies of the blind and vulgar herd, the adamantine walls of the *primum mobile* and the ultimate sphere. Dissolve the notion that our earth is unique and central to the whole . . . to the end that illumined by such contemplation we may proceed with surer steps toward a knowledge of nature."[61] Copernicus advanced a system in which the sun and the earth switch positions, but it remained for Bruno to draw out the implications of a total rearrangement of the solar system.

Bruno had a firm awareness that anyone who put forth ideas must do so apart from what may be held in common opinion by the multitude. This aspect of Bruno's thought struck a chord with James Joyce. In his early essay, "The Day of the Rabblement," the opening line is: "No man, said the Nolan, can be a lover of the true or the good unless he abhors the multitude; and the artist, though he may employ the crowd, is very careful to isolate himself."[62] The philosopher stands in this position, with the artist. The philosopher takes reason wherever it leads. The artist takes imagination wherever it leads. Reason and imagination always lead to thoughts and images that are beyond what is already accepted by the multitude. Bruno brings in a new age as representative of the Renaissance, passing beyond the Scholasticism of the Middle Ages. To philosophize, as also to poeticize, is to make common sense stand on its head and thus to make the multitude confront a world not seen by it before.

---

61   Ibid., 378.
62   Joyce, "Rabblement," 69.

Part Four
Moderns

13

Descartes's Archimedean Point

René Descartes (1596–1650) was born at La Hayne in the Touraine region of France. He was educated at the Jesuit college of La Flèche. In 1614 or 1615 he entered the University of Poitiers, from which he received a *baccalauréat* and a *licence en droit* (law). He began to pursue a career as a military engineer, going to Holland to serve in the army of Maurice of Nassau. He traveled to Germany, and at Ulm he had a sequence of three dreams, which he interpreted as a divine sign that he was to found a unified science of nature. He returned to Paris in 1625; then in 1629 he moved to the Low Countries.

In 1633, when he had a relatively complete version of his metaphysics, physics, and biology, he heard of the condemnation, by the Church in Rome, of Galileo's Copernicanism, which caused him not to publish his philosophy. This decision is in accord with his motto, "*Bene qui Latuit, bene Vixit*" — "He who is well hidden, lives well." He remained in the Low Countries until October 1649, when he accepted an invitation to come to Stockholm to join the circle of scholars at the court of Queen Christina of Sweden. In the severe Swedish winter he fell ill with pneumonia, and died in early 1650.

Descartes is the author of one of the two most well-known statements in the history of philosophy: "I think, therefore I am" stands alongside Socrates's statement concerning the life worth living. In the fourth part of *Discours de la méthode* (1637), Descartes asserts: "*ie pense, donc ie suis.*"[63] He comments: "Observing that this truth '*I am thinking, therefore I exist*' was so firm and sure that all the most extravagant suppositions of the sceptics were incapable of shaking it, I decided that I could accept it without scruple as the first principle of the philosophy I was seeking."[64] In the second meditation of *Meditationes de prima philosophia* (1641),

---

63 Descartes, *Oeuvres*, 6:33.
64 Descartes, *Philosophical Writings*, 1:127.

Descartes says: "*Ego sum, ego existo.*"[65] He prefaces this formulation by saying that even if there is a deceiver of supreme power and cunning, who is constantly deceiving him: "In that case I too undoubtedly exist, if he is deceiving me; and let him deceive me as much as he can, he will never bring it about that I am nothing so long as I think I am something."[66]

Descartes arrives at the certain truth that he exists by his method of hypothetical doubt. He says: "Anything which admits of the slightest doubt I will set aside just as if I had found it to be wholly false; and I will proceed in this way until I recognize something certain, or, if nothing else, until I at least recognize for certain that there is no certainty. Archimedes used to demand just one firm immovable point in order to shift the entire earth [*Nihil nisi punctum petebat Archimedes, quod esset firmum & immobile, ut integram terram loco dimoveret*]; so I too can hope for great things if I manage to find just one thing, however slight, that is certain and unshakeable."[67]

In the first part of the *Principia Philosophiae* (1644), a work in which Descartes intends to present his philosophy as a complete system, we find: "*ego cogito, ergo sum.*"[68] He comments that "this piece of knowledge [*haec cognitio;* or *cette proposition* (French version)] is the first and most certain of all to occur to anyone who philosophizes in an orderly way."[69] Descartes thus begins his philosophy, and to a great extent modern philosophy itself, by a very spare version of the Delphic precept of *Gnothi seauton* (Know thyself). Socrates brings philosophy down from the heavens and into cities and homes. Descartes brings philosophy out of its role in medieval thought as the agent of theology and provides philosophy with its own place to stand.

Descartes's Archimedean, immovable point is his conception of the certainty of the thinking I. Its certainty is confirmed by the fact that any attempt by the I to deny its existence presupposes the I's existence. To attempt such a denial involves the affirmation of a

---

65 Descartes, *Oeuvres*, 7:25.
66 Descartes, *Philosophical Writings*, 2:17.
67 Ibid., 2:16.
68 Descartes, *Oeuvres*, 8:7.
69 Ibid., 9:29.

contradiction: that A and non-A are both true—I exist and deny I exist. The standard source for Archimedes's claim is John Tzetzes's twelfth-century *Book of Histories*. Tzetzes says: "In his Doric dialect, and in its Syracusan variant, he [Archimedes] declared: 'If I have somewhere to stand, I will move the whole earth with my *charistion*.'"[70] A *charistion* was used for weighing, likely a triple-pulley device. Plutarch, in his life of *Marcellus* (Consul of Rome, an experienced military figure), says that Marcellus engaged in a campaign in Sicily, attacking Syracuse with artillery fixed on a high platform, supported by eight galleys fastened together. But its great weight caused a problem for its movement.

Archimedes wrote to Marcellus "that with any given force it was possible to move any given weight; and emboldened, as we are told, by the strength of his demonstration, he declared that, if there were another world, and he could go to it, he could move this." Archimedes demonstrated his claim by selecting a merchant ship that had been dragged with great effort ashore, and placed on board many passengers and freight. Then: "He seated himself at a distance from her, and without any great effort, but quietly setting in motion with his hand a system of compound pulleys, drew her towards him smoothly and evenly, as though she were gliding through the water" (*Marcellus*, 14.8-9).

The version of the Archimedean point that has taken shape in the popular consciousness is that Archimedes said he will move the world with a lever. This version is supported by a mistranslation of the line in Diodorus Siculus, *Library of History*, by Francis R. Walton: "Give me a place to stand and with a lever [*charistion*] I will move the whole world" (26.18). Note that Descartes speaks of Archimedes's demand for only an immovable point. To lift the earth with a lever would require two places—a place for a fulcrum and a place to stand. There is no need for Archimedes to invent a lever. Any ancient stonemason knew how to employ a lever. Archimedes stated the principle of the lever as: "Commensurable magnitudes balance at distances reciprocally proportional to their weights."[71] The devising of the pulley and

---

70 *Greek Mathematical Works*, 2:21.
71 Ibid., 2:209.

the interconnection of pulleys to move huge weight is an act of genius. It is the importance of the pulley to which Archimedes is calling attention.

On November 14, 1640, Descartes wrote a reply to a Dutch Protestant minister, Andreas Colvius, regarding his claim of the certainty of the existence of the I, as stated in his *Discourse on Method*. Descartes says: "I am obliged to you for drawing my attention to the passage of St. Augustine relevant to my *I am thinking, therefore I exist*. I went today to the library of this town [Leiden] to read it, and I do indeed find that he does use it to prove the certainty of our existence. He goes on to show that there is a certain likeness of the Trinity in us, in that we exist, we know that we exist, and we love the existence and the knowledge we have. I, on the other hand, use the argument to show that this *I* which is thinking is an *immaterial substance* with no bodily element. These are two very different things. In itself it is such a simple and natural thing to infer that one exists from the fact that one is doubting that it could have occurred to any writer. But I am very glad to find myself in agreement with St. Augustine, if only to hush the little minds who have tried to find fault with the principle."[72]

We are left with the question of whether Descartes's claim of the certain existence of the I is a truth that is to be grasped immediately by direct intuition, in the way that the axioms of Euclidean geometry can be regarded, or whether it is a kind of syllogism stated in enthymematic form, in which I infer my existence from the fact that I am thinking, with the premiss that whatever thinks must exist. We might regard it as both. It is an axiom that we can immediately affirm. Then, once affirmed, we can form it as a syllogism. It becomes an intellectual version of Archimedes's pulley.

---

72 Descartes, *Philosophical Writings*, 3:159. Descartes's reference is to Augustine, *De Civitate Dei* (bk. 11, cap. 26); cf. *De Trinitate*,10.10.

14

Hobbes's Leviathan

Thomas Hobbes (1588-1679) was born at Westport, a parish of Malmesbury, in Wiltshire, England. In 1608, Hobbes completed his degree at Magdalen Hall, Oxford. He toured the Continent and had a command of French and Italian. In 1628, Hobbes published an English translation of Thucydides's *History of the Peloponnesian Wars*. In another tour of the Continent, from 1634 to 1636, Hobbes may have met Galileo in Italy and Mersenne in Paris. When he returned to England he kept up with the scientific work produced by Mersenne's circle in Paris. He was in disagreement with Descartes and criticized Descartes's *Meditations* in a set of *Objections* (the unsigned "Third Set"), published with the sets of *Objections and Replies* appended to the *Meditations* in 1641. In his ninetieth year, Hobbes continued his work on physics by publishing his *Decameron Physiologicum* (1678). Hobbes died in 1679 and was buried in the cemetery of a small parish church near Hardwick.

Hobbes uses *Leviathan* as the title of his most famous book, thus becoming the first to use this word in a prominent, intellectual sense in English, outside of the literature of biblical criticism. His use of it as a title is extraordinary; perhaps he intends it as a play on a colloquial, figurative use that the word had, referring to a man of vast and formidable power or enormous wealth. Because it is unusual, the title becomes immediately memorable. It is likely that Hobbes hoped the reader would notice that the book was "Printed for Andrew Crooke, at the Green Dragon in St. Pauls Church-yard, 1651." "Leviathan" is from Hebrew *liwyāthān*, a sea monster, a crocodile, a dragon. Its power can be likened to the civil commonwealth joined to the ecclesiastical commonwealth—the Green Dragon in the churchyard. This is an irony that Hobbes would not have missed, if indeed it was not deliberate. The subtitle of his book is "The

Matter, Forme, & Power of a Common-wealth Ecclesiasticall and Civill."

Hobbes commissioned the frontispiece for his book and assisted with its design. At the top margin is the line from the Latin Vulgate, that concludes the description of Leviathan in the forty-first chapter of the Book of Job in the Hebrew Bible: "*Non est potestas Super Terram quae Comparetur ei* [There is no power on Earth that is comparable to it]." The King James Bible, completed in 1611, forty years prior to Hobbes's work, presents the line as: "Upon earth there is not his like." This is the English version, available in Hobbes's time. The Latin third-person demonstrative (*ei*), functioning as both masculine (to him) and neuter (to it), allows Hobbes to merge Leviathan as "it" (a nonhuman) and as "him" (a human) into the "artificial man," an entity that is like a man but is not such. Hobbes could expect the English reader immediately to complete the line with "who is made without fear" from the King James Bible.

In the *Republic*, the ideal state is presented as the individual writ large. The individual becomes just by enacting a harmony among intellect, will, and appetites. The state becomes just by enacting a harmony among the rulers, guardians, and craftsmen. The state and individual correspond. Hobbes's "artificial man" is the biblical Leviathan, whose power has no equal, transposed from a force of nature into a force of state, the "body politique," made by joining under one ruler the civil and the ecclesiastical commonwealths. Nothing makes this duality of state and church more evident than the five sets of images in the lower half of the frontispiece. From left to right, the castle is portrayed opposite the church; the crown opposite a bishop's mitre; the cannon, that operates through the artificial fire of gunpowder, opposite divine lightning, that emits from the thundercloud; the arms, battle flags, and drum of civil conflict opposite the pikes inscribed with the syllogism and with epistemological and metaphysical distinctions rooted in Scholastic debate; and, last, the full battle scene of war is opposite the courtroom scene of canon law.

In the upper half of the frontispiece, this dualism is repeated, with the figure of the artificial man holding a sword in one hand

and a crosier in the other, parallel to the two sets of images of state power and church power. On the head of the figure of the artificial man is a crown. The figure itself is composed of a multitude of individual subjects, looking upward. The figure stands over a representation of town and countryside, absorbing all that there is in his absolute power. The body politic is man-made, that is, it is the artificial Leviathan that is to be feared, but which has no fear.

The meaning of Hobbes's *Leviathan* rests on its relation to the book of Job. The theme of the book of Job is the obedient individual's relation to the immortal power of God. Hobbes's intention in *Leviathan* is to rewrite the book of Job for the gentile nations, for the modern, individual subject. The ancient Hebrews could speak to God directly. The Lord appears to Job in a whirlwind and says: "I will question you, and you shall declare to me" (Job 38:3). They engage in an exchange. God reminds Job of the vastness of divine power that is joined with the vastness of divine wisdom. Ultimately the Lord faces Job with the power of nature itself, in the form of the Leviathan. Job then knows that man is not the measure of all things and that fear of the Lord is the beginning of wisdom (Proverbs 9:10). The rise of modern science has altered the relation of man to himself and to the human ability to command power over the natural world. But unlike the ancients, the moderns face, in the commonwealth, "that *Mortall God*, to which wee owe under the *Immortall God*, our peace and defence."[73]

Hobbes's concern, above all, is the individual subject, who is, as such, powerless against the multitude that is the state. His purpose for the whole book is ultimately to convey advice on how to live within the state, which is not the individual writ large but the multitude formed as the body politic. It matters not whether its government is a democracy, aristocracy, oligarchy, or monarchy. The political subject is a modern Job. Hobbes knows that equality is an ideal. In the state of nature there is no equality. The stronger dominate at will; life for the weaker is "solitary, poore, nasty, brutish, and short."[74]

---

73   Hobbes, *Leviathan*, 227.
74   Ibid., 186.

Once the state of nature is surmounted, the covenant accomplished, and human beings are brought together in a government to secure protection for themselves, the problem emerges, Hobbes says, of "*Why Evill men often Prosper, and Good men suffer Adversity.*"[75] He says this is the problem that governs the book of Job. One form of government may provide better conditions for its subjects than another, but this condition of inequality persists regardless in all human affairs. There is no known political solution for it, just as there is no resolution of Job's afflictions through the arguments of his friends, who arrive to offer advice. No action by any state will fully eliminate it. This is the human condition itself. Hobbes shows inequality to be a permanent feature of life in the body politic.

All this Hobbes knows. His work, when understood, allows us to accept the human condition as a matter of prudence. This acceptance is the lesson Hobbes's *Leviathan* teaches the individual. In addition to its purpose for the survival of the individual, it contains a science of government. Hobbes says: "He that is to govern a whole Nation, must read in himself, not this, or that particular man; but Man-kind." He says this ability is as hard to learn as any language or science. "Yet when I shall have set down my own reading orderly and perspicuously, the pains left another, will be only to consider, if he also find not the same in himself." Hobbes concludes: "For this kind of Doctrine admitteth no other Demonstration."[76] In this way the science of government can be learned. This advice, and the advice Hobbes's work contains for the individual, cannot be overlooked.

Leviathan shows us that politics is not ethics. When politics is assigned the duty to resolve questions of proper conduct among individuals, the private sphere of individual life disappears. Political principles concern the use of power. Ethical principles concern how one human being is to act in relation to another, and such principles cannot be learned by the study or use of politics. Central to ethics is the idea of friendship. True friendship has no place in politics. Leviathan governs by unstated fear, the fear that the individual rightly has of political power.

---

75 Ibid., 398.
76 Ibid., 83.

15

Vico's Poetic Wisdom

Giambattista Vico (1668-1744) was born at Naples. According to his autobiography, he fell headfirst from a ladder at age seven, likely in his father's small bookstore. Having fractured his cranium, he remained unconscious for five hours, causing the surgeon to predict that he would either die or would grow up stolid. Neither part of this prediction came true. According to his autobiography, the fall left him with a melancholy and irritable temperament, which, as he says, is characteristic of persons of ingenuity and depth. Such a temperament is classically associated with philosophers. Vico was largely self-educated—an autodidact. He became professor of Latin Eloquence at the University of Naples in 1699, a position he held until his retirement in 1741. His teaching duties were limited to preparing young students for a career in law.

The decisive event of Vico's career was his failure to succeed in the concourse for a chair of civil law, in 1723. The chair was given to Domenico Gentile whose only attempt at writing a book resulted in it being withdrawn from the press for plagiarism. As a result of the decision of the concourse, Vico decided to abandon writing academic works in Latin, and to devote himself to presenting his original ideas in Italian. The result was his masterpiece, the *Scienza nuova*. Vico died during the night of January 22-23, 1744.

Vico's master work appeared in three editions: in 1725 (known as the *Scienza nuova prima*), and in 1730 and 1744 (known together as the *Scienza nuova seconda*). Vico was seeing the 1744 edition through the press at the time of his death. The full title of this third, definitive edition is *Principj di Scienza Nuova di Giambattista Vico d'intorno alla comune natura delle nazioni* [*Principles of New Science of Giambattista Vico concerning the Common Nature of the Nations*]. Vico's title was inspired by Bacon's *Novum Organum* (his new logic) and Galileo's *Dialoghi delle Nuove Scienze* (Dialogues on the new sciences). Vico's ambition was to formulate a science of human society, or the "world of nations," which would be comparable to the science of nature as produced by such figures as Galileo and Newton. Vico realized that the *idea of law* that is at the basis of the new science of nature is also at the basis of a new science of the world of nations derived from the *ius gentium*, the law common to all peoples, described in the Roman *Digest of Justinian* (1.1.4). By conceiving this law as a series of stages governing the development of all nations, Vico discovered his new science of the human world.

Vico's major predecessor in this aim was Hobbes. But in Vico's view Hobbes lacked an adequate conception of the origin and development of society, as did the seventeenth-century natural-law theorists generally. The world of nations does not originate by means of a covenant or contract rationally agreed to among human beings, forming a government that could limit the powers of the stronger against the weaker and offering to individuals protection for themselves and their property.

Vico says: "We find that the principle of these origins both of languages and letters lies in the fact that the first gentile peoples, by a demonstrated necessity of nature, were poets who spoke in poetic characters. This discovery, which is the master key of this Science, has cost us the persistent research of almost all our literary life, because with our civilized natures we [moderns] cannot at all imagine [*immaginare*] and can understand [*intendere*] only by great toil the poetic nature of these first men."[77] Vico's exposition of this discovery is the subject of the second and largest division of his *New Science*.

Ernst Cassirer, in *The Problem of Knowledge*, says: "Giambattista Vico may be called the real discoverer of the myth. He immersed himself in its motley world of forms and learned by his study that this world has its own peculiar structure and time order and language. He made the first attempts to decipher this

---

[77] Vico, *New Science*, par. 34.

language, gaining a method by which to interpret the 'sacred pictures,' the hieroglyphics of myth."[78] What Cassirer calls "Mythical Thought" (*Das mythische Denken*), the second volume of his *Philosophy of Symbolic Forms*, is what Vico calls "Poetic Wisdom" (*La sapienza poetica*).

Poetic wisdom is accomplished by the first humans through the power of *fantasia*. *Fantasia* (verb: *fantasticare*) is one of two words for imagination in Italian; the other is *immaginazione* (verb: *immaginare*). In Vico's conception of these two words, *immaginazione* is the power of the mind to call something to mind, to visualize something not present. *Fantasia* (which preserves the Greek *phantasia*) is a primordial power of mind to make a truth, or to provide thought with an *arché*, a first principle. Vico says that "memory is the same as imagination [*la memoria è la stessa che la fantasia*]."[79] *Fantasia* is the power to bring forth from memory a *topos*, a place from which to make further thought. It is a divine power to form what was, is, and is to come, the power invested in the Muses by their mother, Mnemosyne. Through *fantasia* we make again what is already made and stored in human memory.

The first poetic character or "imaginative universal" (*universale fantastico*) for the gentile nations is Jove (*Giove*). Jove is a divine character derived from thunder. Jove is "the first human thought in the gentile world—articulate language began to develop by way of onomatopoeia, through which we still find children happily expressing themselves."[80] The first human beings used their *fantasia* to articulate their great passions. These first humans were "all robust bodily strength, who expressed their very violent passions by shouting [*urlando*] and grumbling [*brontolando*], they pictured the sky to themselves as a great animated body, which in that aspect they called Jove, the first god of the so-called greater gentes, who meant to tell them something

---

78   Cassirer, *Problem of Knowledge*, 296.
79   Vico, *New Science*, par. 819.
80   Ibid., par. 447.

by the hiss of his bolts and the clap of his thunder."[81] *Urlare* is the verb for both a howl of an animal and the shout of a human. *Brontolare* is the verb designating both to grumble and to rumble (as of thunder).

Vico says: "Human words were formed next from interjections which are sounds articulated under the impetus of violent passions. In all languages these are monosyllables. Thus it is not beyond likelihood that, when wonder [*meraviglia*] had been awakened in men by the first thunderbolts, these interjections of Jove should give birth to one produced by the human voice: *pa!*; and that this should then be doubled: *pape!*" From this interjection of the human voice, imitating the sound of thunder, "was subsequently derived Jove's title of father of men and gods, and thus it came about presently that all the gods were called fathers and the goddesses, mothers."[82] Once the human mind acquires the power to name one thing, it has the power to name all things. All gentile nations have a common origin: "For every gentile nation had its Jove."[83]

One of Vico's axioms states: "Doctrines must take their beginning from that of the matters of which they treat."[84] Thus a science of the common nature of the nations must begin where the nations themselves all begin. This science is a science of the civil world and a science of history, because the civil world develops in terms of what Vico calls "ideal eternal history" (*storia ideal eterna*), his transformation of the *ius gentium*, as mentioned above, into a conception of three ages, though which each nation, at its own pace, passes. These three ages are: an age of gods, in which all of nature is ordered in terms of a pantheon of deities; an age of heroes, in which society expresses human virtue through heroic figures, such as Achilles and Ulysses; and an age of humans, in which social order depends on written laws and rational

---

81   Ibid., par. 377.
82   Ibid., par. 448.
83   Ibid., par. 380.
84   Ibid., par. 314 (axiom 106).

procedures. This common history is governed by providence. But no nation overcomes history. All nations rise and fall within history. This ideal eternal history is "traversed in time by every nation in its rise, development, maturity, decline, and fall."[85]

Vico says: "Men first feel necessity, then look for utility, next attend to comfort. still later amuse themselves with pleasure, thence grow dissolute in luxury, and finally go mad and waste their substance [*finalmente impazzano in istrappazzar le sostanze*]."[86] The great city of nations is founded and governed by God. But when a nation devolves from its original piety to Jove, and "if the peoples are rotting in that ultimate civil disease and cannot agree on a monarch from within, and are not conquered and preserved by better nations from without, then providence for their extreme ill has its extreme remedy at hand." A nation, having reached a state comparable to the lowest level of Dante's *Inferno* — the level of fraud and treachery — is "made more inhuman by the barbarism of reflection than the first men had been made by the barbarism of sense."[87] Providence then allows the nation to attempt a retrial, a *ricorso*, and the stages of ideal eternal history begin again.

Vico says: "But in the night of thick darkness enveloping the earliest antiquity, so remote from ourselves, there shines the eternal and never failing light of a truth beyond all question: that the world of civil society has certainly been made by men, and that its principles are therefore to be found within the modifications of our own human mind."[88] Because we are the makers of the civil world and history, we can make a knowledge of it. It is an art of self-knowledge. Vico says: "Indeed, we make bold to affirm that he who mediates [*meditare*] this Science narrates [*narrare*] to himself this ideal eternal history so far as he himself makes it for himself by that proof 'it had, has, and will

---

85 Ibid., par. 245.
86 Ibid., par. 241 (axiom 66).
87 Ibid., par. 1106.
88 Ibid., par. 331.

have to be' [*dovette, deve, dovrà*]. . . . And history cannot be more certain than when he who creates the things also narrates them."[89]

Vico's proof is a modification of the power of the Muses. The Muses tell us of what was, is, and is to come. Vico recasts this sequence as a sequence of necessity—had, has, and will have to be. What is cannot be changed. Vico's last sentence in the *New Science* is: "To sum up, from all that we have set forth in this work, it is to be finally concluded that this Science carries inseparably with it the study of piety, and that he who is not pious cannot be truly wise."[90] History has a providential order and cannot be other than it is. We can act prudently once we grasp this providential order that is present in all things.

---

89 Ibid., par. 349.
90 Ibid., par. 1112.

16

Rousseau's Promethean Discourse

Jean-Jacques Rousseau (1712-1778) was born in Geneva, Switzerland, the second son of Isaac Rousseau, watchmaker. His mother died a few days after his birth. He rose to become one of the best-known figures of the French Enlightenment. He also became a critic of much of the ideals of that period. The turning-point in his life was in July, 1749, when he read in a newspaper of an essay competition of the Academy of Dijon, concerning whether advances in the sciences and arts—the great interests of the Enlightenment—had tended to improve morals. Rousseau claimed that the rest of his life's work was determined from that moment. But he also claimed that he regretted taking up a career in letters.

His great interest was music. In the 1740s he composed a number of operas which had some success. The best-known of the operas is *Le Devin du Village* ("The Village Soothsayer"). He also wrote a *Dictionary of Music* (1767). Rousseau's masterpiece of educational theory is *Émile* (1762), and *The Social Contract* (1762) is his masterpiece of political theory. A section of *Émile* was judged unacceptable by the religious authorities. In fear of imprisonment, Rousseau fled Paris in June, 1762. In 1770 he returned to Paris and was then a celebrated figure. Between 1764 and 1775 he wrote his *Confessions*, which were published posthumously. He died at Ermenonville in June, 1778.

What has become known as Rousseau's "First Discourse" (1750) was written in response to the question proposed by the Academy of Dijon, and for it Rousseau was awarded the prize. The question the Academy proposed was: "*Si le rétablissement des Sciences et des Arts a contribué à épurer les moeurs* [If the restoration of the sciences and arts has tended to purify morals]." This question recalls the myth that Prometheus stole fire from Hephaestus to equip the human race with a means for survival, as fire offers access to the practical arts. But this gift was not accompanied by the wisdom needed for humans to live together in society, that is, political wisdom, including manners (*manières*) and morals (*moeurs*).

The *locus classicus* for this story is in Plato's *Protagoras* (320d–22d). There was a time when the gods existed but mortal beings did not. At the proper moment in the genesis of things, the gods moulded the various forms of these beings inside the earth. When the gods were ready to bring these beings into the world, they put Prometheus and his brother, Epimetheus, in charge of assigning to each type its particular powers and abilities. Epimetheus (whose name means "afterthought," i.e., heedless) begged Prometheus (whose name means "forethought") to grant him the privilege of distributing powers and abilities among the various species. It was agreed that Epimetheus could do so, but that, once done, Prometheus would inspect it.

When Epimetheus was finished, Prometheus discovered that Epimetheus had equipped all the species of animals with means for their survival. To some he assigned wings, to others the means to burrow underground. For protection against the weather he gave some thick pelts and hides. He shod some with hooves and gave others claws. He also provided them with various forms of nourishment. All the species, including humans, were released into the light from inside the earth. Only human beings were left naked, exposed to the elements with no natural means for their survival. This caused Prometheus to give them fire, which was rightly the possession of only the gods. For this theft, Zeus chained Prometheus to the Caucasus Mountains and caused an eagle to come, every third day, to gnaw his liver. This torture continued for age-long centuries, until Zeus finally retracted the punishment.

Zeus feared that, because human beings did not possess the art of politics, they might scatter and be destroyed, unable to form cities. He sent Hermes to distribute equally to all humans the virtue of justice, joined with the proper sense of shame. The Academy's question asks whether there has been progress in the ability of human beings to live virtuously, politically equal to their ability to live well physically. Ernst Cassirer says, in his compact treatise, *The Question of Jean-Jacques Rousseau*: "Indeed, the first *Discours* appears as a rhetorical masterpiece unsurpassed in the whole of Rousseau's writings. . . . No matter how we feel about it and about the single steps of Rousseau's argumentation, the truthfulness of Rousseau's inner sentiment impresses itself upon us in every sentence of the *Discours*." Cassirer says: "Rousseau's ethics [*Ethik*] resolves itself into this one fundamental idea and feeling."[91]

The fundamental idea and feeling to which Cassirer is referring is Rousseau's conclusion to his *Discourse*: "O virtue! sublime science of simple souls [*des âmes simples*]. . . . Are not your principles engraved in all our hearts, and is it not enough in order to learn your laws to commune with oneself and listen to the voice of one's conscience in the silence of the passions? That is true philosophy [*Voilà la véritable Philosophie*], let us know how to be satisfied with it."[92] Rousseau's theme is that: "Our souls have been corrupted in proportion to the advancement of our sciences and arts toward perfection."[93] Rousseau says: "I want to remain what I am."[94] He says: "Thus the dissolution of morals, a necessary consequence of luxury, leads in turn to the corruption of taste [*goût*]."[95] He says: "Luxury rarely develops without the sciences and arts, and they never develop without it."[96] And he says: "Among us, it is true, Socrates would not have drunk the hemlock; but he would have drunk from an even more bitter cup: insulting ridicule and scorn a hundred times worse than death."[97]

Rousseau offers a concise picture of human society as it moved toward the present day: "When innocent and virtuous

---

91 Cassirer, *Jean-Jacques Rousseau*, 48.
92 Rousseau, *Discourses*, 64.
93 Ibid., 39.
94 Ibid., 44.
95 Ibid., 53.
96 Ibid., 50.
97 Ibid., 46.

men enjoyed having gods as witnesses of their actions, they lived together in the same huts; but soon becoming evil, they tired of these inconvenient spectators and relegated them to magnificent temples. Finally, they chased the gods out in order to live in the temples themselves, or at least the temples of the gods were no longer distinguishable from the houses of citizens."[98]

The problem contained in the Prometheus myth has not been reduced, it has instead become increasingly intense. The Enlightenment belief in progress is the result of false philosophy. Such philosophy gives us "in a word, the semblance of all the virtues without the possession of any."[99] Rousseau says: "How pleasant it would be to live among us if exterior appearance were always a reflection of the heart's disposition; if decency were virtue; if our maxims served as our rules; if true philosophy were inseparable from the title of philosopher!"[100] He says, further: "Whoever wants to praise the sobriety of the wise men [*des Sages*] of our day may do so; as for me, I see in it only a refinement of intemperance as unworthy of my praise as their cunning simplicity."[101]

False philosophy is that which proceeds to explain and to justify critically the success of the sciences and arts, showing how much we have gained from them. True philosophy is an activity of the soul's discourse with itself in the attempt to discover what it is to be human. Rousseau's philosophy is neo-Socratic. As he says in the opening paragraph of his *Discourse*: "Which side should I take in this question? The one, gentlemen, that suits an honorable man who knows nothing and yet does not think any less of himself."[102]

The key to Rousseau's conception of philosophy is given in the epigraph he affixed to the title page: "*Barbarus hic ego sum quia non intelligor illis* [Here I am the barbarian, because no one

---

98 Ibid., 54.
99 Ibid., 36.
100 Ibid., 37.
101 Ibid., 38.
102 Ibid., 34.

understands me]" —Ovid's description of himself in exile, in his *Tristia*. In his *Rousseau Juge de Jean-Jacques*, Rousseau considers this epigraph the clue to his entire work. He says, addressing d'Alembert: "*Croyez-vous qu'il se trouve dans l'univers un mortel assez impudent pour dire que c'est J. J.?*"[103] That is, do you think there is to be found in the universe a mortal impudent enough to say that he is J. J.? Ovid is in exile from Rome for his *Ars amatoria*; Rousseau, "A Citizen of Geneva," as he identifies himself as author on the title page of his *Discourse*, is in exile from the Republic of Letters, in which he should have a rightful place. Ovid, poet and speaker of Latin, ordered into exile at Tomis, on the Black Sea, found himself as if a barbarian, in a world of full-blooded barbarians, who went about armed, dressed in skins, with long hair and beards.

Ovid reports: "I must make myself understood by gestures. . . . The Getae laugh stupidly at Latin words, and in my presence they often talk maliciously about me" (5.10.35–39). Ovid says that they even think he may be poking fun at them by speaking Latin, and this reaction can put him in danger. Rousseau realizes that when one finds oneself in such a position there is very little one can do. One cannot be what one is not. One can only hope to overcome the exile by, if necessary, remaining in obscurity, along with common men (*hommes vulgaires*). But among these common men are those *âmes simples* in whom Rousseau must largely place the reception of his work. His audience contains the many and the few. The few are those who know and are in obscurity, or partial obscurity, as ordinary citizens who, like Rousseau, are the descendants of Socratic thinking. These are the readers on whom Rousseau must rely.

---

103 Rousseau, *Oeuvres*, 1:941.

17

Kant's Schematism

Immanuel Kant (1724-1804) was born in Königsberg, the capital of East Prussia, now Kaliningrad, Russia, on the Baltic Sea. He was raised in a household of devout Pietism, a Lutheran revival movement dedicated to simplicity of worship and individual access to God. At age sixteen Kant entered the University of Königsberg. He left the University in 1746. After publishing several scientific works and completing his Master's thesis, he returned to the University as *Privatdozent* and began lecturing in 1755, offering courses on logic, metaphysics, ethics, and physics, as well as on physical geography, anthropology, pedagogy, and fortifications. He was appointed Professor of Logic and Metaphysics in 1770. Crown Prince Frederick, on a visit, remarked that the University of Königsberg was more suited "to the training of bears than to becoming a theatre of the sciences."[104] Kant retired from teaching in 1797, at age seventy-three. He died in Königsberg in 1804.

Kant's most famous work, *Kritik der reinen Vernunft* (*Critique of Pure Reason*, 1st. ed. 1781; 2d ed. 1787), is a masterpiece of making philosophical distinctions. Making such distinctions is the basis of critical thought. In a long footnote to the "Preface to First Edition," Kant says: "Our age is, in especial degree, the age of criticism [*Kritik*], and to criticism everything must submit."[105] In this work the reader enters what we may call the enormous Platonic-like cave of experience, in which thought is thinking through all the various senses of its activity.

The cave of experience holds them all, for as Kant says in the first sentence of his work: "There can be no doubt that all our

---

104 Klinke, *Kant*, 17.
105 Kant, *Critique*, 9n.

knowledge begins with experience."[106] He also says: "Experience is therefore our first instruction, and in its progress is so inexhaustible in new information, that in the interconnected lives of all future generations there will never be any lack of new knowledge that can be thus ingathered."[107] Kant is a thinker of the German Enlightenment (*Aufklärung*). The great cave of experience encloses all that is accessible to the Understanding (*Verstand*). Our efforts to bring forth its contents will be greeted by progress.

The reader is first shown the distinction between analytic and synthetic judgments. "Analytic judgments (affirmative) are therefore those in which the connection of the predicate with the subject is thought through identity; those in which this connection is thought without identity should be entitled synthetic." Furthermore: "Judgments of experience, as such, are one and all synthetic."[108] After this distinction, accompanied by the subdistinctions of *a priori* and *a posteriori*, the reader, taken through the Transcendental Aesthetic of space and time, is shown the Table of Categories, which correspond to the twelve types of cognitive judgment. And in regard to these pure concepts of the understanding, the reader encounters their deduction. Deduction here, Kant says, refers not to logical deduction but to legal deduction, the demand of *quid juris*—by what right such concepts can be allowed to circulate.

The reader, however, is issued a warning that there are also in experience usurpatory concepts (*usurpierte Begriffe*) that circulate without proper justification: "But there are also usurpatory concepts, such as *fortune* [*Glück*], *fate* [*Schicksal*], which, though allowed to circulate by almost universal indulgence, are yet from time to time challenged by the question: *quid juris*."[109] Kant says these two concepts and their like have no legal title to justify their existence that is obtainable from either experience or

---

106 Ibid., 41.
107 Ibid.
108 Ibid., 48–49.
109 Ibid., 120.

reason. Although Kant does not put it in these terms, fortune and fate, as elements of the human condition, being the frequent subjects of poetry, should be banished, like the poets in the *Republic*. There is no place in the realm of the understanding for such intruders into the world of its justified concepts.

Next, the reader encounters the schematism of the pure concepts of the understanding. The question that has been growing in the reader's mind is: How are these concepts connected to what is perceived in experience by the senses — what Kant calls "intuition" (*Anschauung*)? The reader then learns that this connection is accomplished by the faculty of "imagination" (*Einbildungskraft*), the product or form of which is the *schema*. The schema is not as such an image but is at once sensible and conceptual. The question the reader has now is: What is this extraordinary and crucial element that makes all knowledge possible? Kant says: "This schematism of our understanding, in its application to appearances and their mere form, is an art concealed in the depths of the human soul [*ist eine verborgene Kunst in den Tiefen der menschlichen Seele*], whose real modes of activity nature is hardly likely ever to allow us to discover, and to have open to our gaze."[110]

The reader may be astounded. All of the *Critique*'s doctrine of the understanding, its epistemology, depends upon an art concealed in the human soul, with no expectation that its nature will likely ever emerge. It rivals the other unknowable upon which the *Critique* rests — the thing-in-itself (*Ding-an-sich*). As Kant says, in the "Preface to Second Edition," the reader must bear in mind that our thought must be limited to objects of experience and "that though we cannot *know* these objects as things in themselves, we must yet be in position at least to *think* them as things in themselves; otherwise we should be landed in the absurd conclusion that there can be appearance without anything that appears."[111]

---

110 Ibid., 183.
111 Ibid., 27.

Knowledge takes place through an element that is unknown, based on an object the true nature of which is also unknown, concealed from sense as well as from thought. These things in themselves are noumena, of which there can never be an intuition, a perception. Thus: "It follows that the employment of the categories can never extend further than to the objects of experience."[112] These noumena are the causes of the phenomena that comprise experience, yet the category of cause does not apply to them.

Umberto Eco says, in *Kant and the Platypus*: "As far as Kant is concerned, nature is before our eyes, and his native realism prevents him from thinking that the objects of nature are not there, functioning in a certain way, given that they develop by themselves." A tree, for example, grows as an individual entity by its own internal organic law. "But what this law is cannot be known from the tree, given that the phenomenal teaches us nothing about the noumenal. Nor do the a priori forms of the pure intellect teach us anything, because the entities of nature obey a plethora of particular laws." How do we know with specificity what things truly are? "These objects of nature are (apart from those highly general laws that allow us to think of the phenomena of physics) dogs, horses, stones—and platypuses." We must simply imagine something as possible according to the concept. "And so we try to construct the concept of tree (we assume it) *as if* the trees were as we can think them."[113] We do not learn, from Kant's transcendental method, how we know a dog is a dog, or a cat a cat.

The reader, having been guided by Kant through this great cave of experience, is now shown that within it is an island where all is pure and perfect. This is the territory of pure understanding. Beyond it is the treacherous territory of pure reason, of speculative thinking about what the self is in itself, or the world is in itself, or whether God exists. To pursue thought beyond

---

112 Ibid., 270.
113 Eco, *Kant and the Platypus*, 91.

experience, to attempt to reach these objects, is to involve the mind in the dialectic of arguments pro and con, to which there are no resolutions. As with fortune and fate, there is no *quid juris* available. This realization should cause the reader to resist the temptations that the speculative use of reason holds, and to accept a regime of self-discipline, of thinking only within experience. Kant says: "If in the speculative employment of pure reason there are no dogmas, to serve as its special subject-matter, all *dogmatic* methods, whether borrowed from the mathematician or specially invented, are as such inappropriate."[114] All thought should be a reflection on what is in experience. Metaphysics must be a metaphysics of experience, nothing more.

Kant's description of this island is the only poetic passage in all of the *Critique*. It takes the reader to the limits of the understanding. The island provides the reader with an image of how to live and think wholly within experience. It replaces the sense of the great cave, in which the reader has been wandering. Like Robinson Crusoe, we must learn how to conduct ourselves on this island. Kant says: "We have now not merely explored the territory of pure understanding, and carefully surveyed every part of it, but have also measured its extent, and assigned to everything in it its rightful place." Now that this assessment is complete, we can see that: "This domain is an island, enclosed by nature itself within unalterable limits. It is the land of truth—enchanting name!—surrounded by a wide and stormy ocean, the native home of illusion, where many a fog bank and many a swiftly melting iceberg give the deceptive appearance of farther shores, deluding the adventurous seafarer ever anew with empty hopes, and engaging him in enterprises which he can never abandon and yet is unable to carry to completion."[115]

Our arrival at the "land of truth" carries with it a stern warning of the danger of speculative thinking, of thought attempting to think itself and drift off into the realm of

---

114 Kant, *Critique*, 592.
115 Ibid., 257.

contemplation, in which thought can never be finalized. There is enough to do right here on the island.

18

Hegel's Speculative Sentence

Georg Wilhelm Friedrich Hegel (1770-1831) was born in Stuttgart, Germany. Following grammar school, he entered a course of study at the Protestant Seminary in Tübingen, in preparation for a career as a Protestant clergyman. Schelling and Hölderlin, who also were students in the Tübingen Seminary, became Hegel's friends. In 1793, after completing this period of study, Hegel became a private tutor in Berne, Switzerland, and following that became a private tutor in Frankfurt am Main. Early in 1801 he went to Jena, where Schelling was lecturing in philosophy at the University. Schelling supported Hegel's appointment as *Privatdozent*. To attain this position, Hegel submitted a Latin dissertation on the orbits of the planets—*Dissertatio philosophica de Orbitis Planetarum*—twenty-five pages in length.

In his first real publication, the so-called *Differenzschrift*, concerning the systems of Fichte and Schelling, Hegel identified himself on the title page as "Doctor of Worldly Wisdom [*der Weltweisheit Doktor*]." After Napoleon's capture of Jena, Hegel left the University, and in 1807 became editor of a daily newspaper in Bramberg. In 1808 he became rector and professor at a grammar school in Nurenberg. In 1816 he accepted a professorship at the University of Heidelberg, and in 1818 he left to take a chair, as Fichte's successor, at the University of Berlin. Hegel died in Berlin during a cholera epidemic in 1831.

Hegel's system, as he originally conceived it, is in two parts: *System der Wissenschaft: Erster Teil, die Phänomenologie des Geistes* (*System of Science: First Part, the Phenomenology of Spirit*) (1807) and *Wissenschaft der Logik* (*Science of Logic*), which was published in three volumes in 1812, 1813, and 1816. His other two book-length works are *Enzyklopädie der philosophischen Wissenschaften im Grundrisse. Zum Gebrauch seiner Vorlesungen* (*Encyclopedia of the Philosophical Sciences in Outline. For Use with His Lectures*) (1817, reprinted in two completely revised editions in 1827 and 1830). This work has sometimes been mistaken for the statement of Hegel's system, but it is a textbook expressing his ideas in a simplified form. His title of *Enzyklopädie* may be intended as a play on the great Enlightenment *Encyclopédie* of D'Alembert and Diderot that presents topics alphabetically and not, as Hegel does, systematically.

His fourth book, *Naturrecht und Staatswissenschaft im Grundrisse. Zum Gebrauch für seine Vorlesungen: Grundlinien der Philosophie des Rechts* (*Natural Law and Political Science in Outline: Basic Principles of the Philosophy of Right*) (1821) is an expansion of sections of the *Encyclopedia*. These four books were followed — posthumously — by four volumes of Hegel's lectures on the history of philosophy, philosophy of history, philosophy of religion, and philosophy of fine art — compiled from lecture notes. Not since Aristotle has there been a mind as comprehensive as Hegel's. These works offer their reader a complete philosophical education.

Hegel's most lively work is the *Phenomenology of Spirit*. It is also widely regarded as the most difficult work to read in the history of philosophy. The philosopher and the literary writer face the common problem — how to put thought into words, for both philosophy and literature ultimately depend upon linguistic style — how words can be made to accommodate reason and imagination. The Hegel scholar John Findlay says: "An afflatus seized Hegel in the Jena lecture-rooms, an afflatus perhaps unique in philosophical history, which affected not only his ideas but his style, and which makes one at times only sure that he is saying something immeasurably profound and important, but not exactly what it is."[116] Findlay compares Hegel's genius in this regard to such figures as Shakespeare, Rimbaud, and Mallarmé.

The master key to Hegel's thought is what Hegel, in the Preface to the *Phenomenology of Spirit*, calls the "speculative sentence" (*spekulativer Satz*). Hegel explains this sentence in

---

116 Findlay, "Foreword," xiii.

musical terms. In the speculative sentence the locus of its meaning is first in the subject of the sentence, but to apprehend the meaning of the subject we must pass to the predicate. Once the predicate is grasped, however, we must ask how it is connected back to the subject. The sentence thus has a "floating center." Hegel likens this movement back and forth to rhythm. This rhythm of the opposition between subject and predicate results in an expression of their union. As Hegel says, "Their union [*Einheit*] is supposed to emerge as a harmony."[117]

The difference between subject and predicate is not overcome by their union in the sense of a synthesis or an identity. This union is that of a correspondence between subject and predicate. They are *entsprechend*—matched to each other. As we pass from subject to predicate, and back from predicate to subject, their opposition is taken up within the subject. The inner form of the original opposition of the sentence now becomes the inner form of the subject itself, which can be brought forth as a new predication of the meaning of the subject. The subject's original self-identity is dissolved into an internal, self-dialectical movement. The speculative sentence is the means by which the self can come to know itself.

This dialectical movement of the self's inner form is captured in the German verb *aufheben*. This verb has no real English equivalent. It is often translated as "sublate," as derived from the Latin *sublatus*, to "take away," "lift up." Hegel says that *aufheben* is "at the same time a *negating* and a *preserving* [*es ist ein Negieren und ein Aufbewahren zugleich*]."[118] This German verb, unlike "sublation," is a word of ordinary speech. In the speculative sentence the predicate negates the subject, but the essence of the subject is taken up and preserved in a new formulation of the subject.

Speculative or dialectical thinking depends, not on reflection, but on recollection. The speculative sentence is a memory

---

117 Hegel, *Phenomenology*, par. 61.
118 Ibid., par. 113.

structure. As thought passes from the subject to the predicate, the subject must be remembered and placed in connection with the predicate, and then, when passing back from predicate to subject, the remembered subject-developed predicate must be remembered in the newly apprehended or re-apprehended subject. As consciousness passes back upon itself, through the circle of the speculative sentence, consciousness turns itself into a theater of memory. In so doing, the world as object is remade in speculative speech. The reader who can follow this speech makes a proof in the reader's own mind of that which is claimed. In so doing, the reader moves toward the divine vision of the True as the whole. The whole is composed of all the images formed by these dialectical speech acts. This grasp of the whole is an absolute knowing. To possess absolute knowing (*absolutes Wissen*) is to possess absolute recollection, a total act of self-knowing, a total recall.

As we look through Hegel's *Phenomenology* we encounter what Hegel calls a "Gallery of Images" (*Galerie von Bildern*). We first meet up with a stage of "sense-certainty," a stage in which the whole world is a collection of moments of sensation. We come to the inverted world (*verkehrte Welt*), in which consciousness goes into a swoon—not able to think the difference between the North and South poles, or the difference between criminals and saints. There is the dialectic of master and servant (*Herrschaft und Knechtschaft*) and the unhappy or misfortunate consciousness (*unglückliches Bewußtsein*) as well as the false doctrine of mind, embodied in craniology (*Schädellehre*). There are stances taken by the self, such as the "law of the heart" (*das Gesetz des Herzens*) followed by the "spiritual menagerie" (*das geistige Tierreich*), where everyone is busy with a task of their own self-interest, and the "beautiful soul" (*die schöne Seele*), as well as the state into which society can fall, that of "absolute freedom and terror" (*die absolute Freiheit und der Schrecken*).

Through these images the self is able to see itself as a series of human phenomena, of types of existence. This gallery of images is also a gallery of ironies. Each stage of Hegel's "science of the experience of consciousness" begins in the belief that consciousness can unify itself, only to realize that the attempt to bring consciousness into a unity with itself is an illusion. The irony is that we cannot stabilize consciousness to form a whole. It keeps separating itself into various stages, one stage leading to another. The self looks at itself one way, and then it finds yet another way to look at itself.

No one without a sense of humor can read Hegel's works. Bertolt Brecht says Hegel "had the stuff of one of the greatest humorists among philosophers. Socrates is the only other one who had a similar method. . . . It was clear to him that right next to the greatest order dwells the greatest disorder. . . . What order affirms, disorder, its inseparable partner, opposes at once, in one breath where possible. They can neither live without one another nor with one another. . . . I have never met a person without a sense of humor who has understood Hegel's dialectic."[119] Speculative philosophy knows that all truths are partial errors and all errors are partial truths. This realization is reached only through a sense of irony. Hegel teaches us to realize the error of taking ourselves seriously. Attributed to Oscar Wilde is the claim that all bad poetry is sincere. We may say, of philosophy, that all bad philosophy is sincere. Sincere philosophy is literal-minded — philosophy that separates reason from irony and the imagination.

Looking at many of the great texts, from Plato to Hegel, we see how speculative philosophy is written, and can be written. They defy us to reduce philosophy to no more than arguments pro and con — the instruments of literal-mindedness. These great figures direct us to the possibilities of a wisdom that includes the vivacity of the image and the presence of doubt that is inherent in the question. These possibilities are the medium of a philosophic spirit.

---

119 Brecht, *Flüchtlingsgespräche*, 108–11. My trans.

19

Cassirer's Symbolic Forms

Ernst Cassirer (1874–1945) was born in Breslau, Silesia, now Wroclaw, Poland. He studied at the universities of Berlin, Leipzig, Heidelberg, and Marburg. At Marburg, Cassirer became a disciple of the neo-Kantian philosopher, Hermann Cohen. Cassirer's doctoral dissertation, written under Cohen, became part of his first book, *Leibniz' System* (1902). Cassirer first taught at Berlin. He then went to a professorship at Hamburg, from 1919 to 1933. He served as rector there from 1930 to 1933. With the rise of National Socialism, Cassirer resigned his position, going first to All Souls, at Oxford University, from 1933 to 1935, where he lectured on Hegel, then to Göteborg, Sweden, from 1935 to 1941. He came to Yale University in 1941. Cassirer died suddenly on his way to class, while on a visiting professorship at Columbia University, in the spring of 1945.

The critical edition of Cassirer's published writings is in twenty-five volumes. In addition, the manuscripts of his *Nachlass* occupy eighteen volumes, including a volume of his correspondence. At the center of Cassirer's thought are his multi-volume history of modern philosophy, *Das Erkenntnisproblem in der Philosophie und Wissenschaft der neueren Zeit* (The problem of knowledge in philosophy and science in the modern age), and the multi-volume work of his systematic philosophy, *The Philosophy of Symbolic Forms*.

Cassirer regards the problem of knowledge to be the central concern of modern philosophy as it developed from Descartes through Kant to Hegel and the epistemologies presupposed in physics, biology, and history since Hegel. As discussed above in the chapter on Kant, Kant brings the problem of knowledge to the problem of the schematism. The schema is the means through which the concepts of the understanding acquire content as supplied by the senses. As mentioned above, Kant tells the reader of the *Critique of Pure Reason* that this schematism of the understanding "is an art concealed in the depths of the human soul, whose real modes of activity nature is hardly likely ever to allow us to discover, and have open to our gaze."[120] Kant shows that all knowledge requires something that is at once conceptual and perceptible. But Kant is unable to show us what this twofold thing is.

Cassirer finds Kant's principle of the schematism fully present in the unique human possession of the symbol. As he says in *An Essay of Man*, the human being is *animal symbolicum*. This term replaces the classical definition of the human being as *animal rationale*.[121] The human being is the only animal that can give an account of its existence. This account is based on the human power of the symbol to produce culture. The symbol takes shape in its various cultural forms, such as myth, religion, language, art, history, and science. By transposing the idea of the schematism into the phenomenon of the symbolic form, Cassirer moves the problem of knowledge beyond Kant. Cassirer says: "Thus the critique of reason becomes the critique of culture. It seeks to understand and to show how every content of culture, in so far as it is more than a mere isolated content, in so far as it is grounded in a universal principle of form, presupposes an original act of the human spirit."[122]

Cassirer considers philosophical idealism as having its origin in Plato's doctrine of ideas. Cassirer says: "In order to delimit the 'sphere' of the word from the sphere of pure concepts, and at the same time to maintain the connection between them, Plato now need only invoke the central principle of the theory of ideas, the principle of 'participation.'"[123] The problem of how the ideas or forms, which make things what they are in the world and which can be thought through words, are connected to things as

---

120 Kant, *Critique*, 183.
121 Cassirer, *Essay*, 26.
122 Cassirer, *Philosophy of Symbolic Forms*, 1:80.
123 Ibid., 1:125.

perceived, is left unresolved by Plato. It becomes the abiding problem of philosophical idealism over the centuries. Kant's version of the problem of participation is the connection of concepts with sensible "intuitions" in the schematism.

The term "symbolic form" (*symbolische Form*) is distinctive to Cassirer's philosophical idealism. Cassirer defines this term as: "Under a 'symbolic form' should be understood each energy of spirit [*Energie des Geistes*] through which a spiritual content or meaning is connected with a concrete sensory sign and is internally adapted to this sign."[124] A symbolic form has an internal bond between a universal meaning and the particular sensory sign in which the meaning inheres. A symbol is at once inseparably "spiritual" (*geistig*) and "sensible" (*sinnlich*).

Cassirer advances a phenomenological proof of how symbolic form is grounded in the stances consciousness can take on the object.[125] His example is a *Linienzug*, or graph-like line drawing. Cassirer asks us to consider a first apprehension of the line drawing as an object having purely sensory qualities, such that we grasp the tension in its shape, feel its motion, and so forth. Then we may shift our perspective and regard the line as a mathematical object, as perhaps a figure showing various proportions. Putting aside these two different formations of the meaning of the object, we may regard it as a mythical-magical form, as a sign that divides a sacred from a profane sphere. We may pass from this meaning to apprehending it as an aesthetic ornament, appreciating its artistic properties purely for their own sake. This experiment confirms Cassirer's theory of the symbol as simultaneously *geistig* and *sinnlich*. We do not simply sense the object and then regard it as representing a concept. The essence of the object is present in its immediate apprehension.

Cassirer claims that "it is a common characteristic of all symbolic forms that they are applicable to any object

---

124 Cassirer, "Der Begriff der symbolische Form," 175. My trans.
125 Cassirer, *Philosophy of Symbolic Forms*, 3:200-202.

whatsoever."[126] Thus if we were to continue to apprehend the line drawing, we could form it as having a legal and social or ethical significance, or as an economic object or an instance of technology, or as a historical artifact.[127] All the various ways in which the object can be apprehended are writ large in the symbolic forms of human culture. In speaking about symbols we are accustomed to make a distinction between what is symbolic and what is literal. Cassirer's epistemology rejects this distinction. Whatever might be designated as literal is, in Cassirer's view, another symbolic formation of experience. The literal is thus itself symbolic. One formation of experience is not more "symbolic" than another. The symbol is the medium of all human experience and hence the medium of all formations of it. Each way of apprehending the object has its own inner form (*innere Form*). It is the aim of Cassirer's philosophy of culture to elicit these inner forms—the internal logic of myth, religion, art, history, science, and so forth.

Philosophy is not a symbolic form that stands alongside the other symbolic forms. Cassirer says: "It is characteristic of philosophical knowledge as the 'self-knowledge' of reason that it does not create a principally new symbol form, it does not found in this sense a new creative modality—but it grasps the earlier modalities as that which they are, as characteristic symbolic forms."[128] Philosophy does not have a formation of the object distinct to itself. What philosophy can know of the object derives from its grasp of what the symbolic forms that make up culture provide.

Cassirer regards culture as a dialectically ordered whole, as a coexistence of contraries. He describes this whole through a line of Heraclitus: "'Men do not understand,' said Heraclitus, 'how that which is torn in different directions comes into accord with itself—harmony in contrariety, as in the case of the bow and the

---

126 Cassirer, *Myth of the State*, 34.
127 Cassirer, *Philosophy of Symbolic Forms*, 2:xiv–xv.
128 Cassirer, *Philosophy of Symbolic Forms*, 4:226.

lyre.'"[129] *Harmonia*, in this line of Heraclitus, calls attention to the fact that the strings connect the bow and the lyre each to themselves. The line also suggests that the bow and the lyre perform opposite functions but depend upon the same power to do so — the tension of the strings. We cannot experience one opposite without the other.

The hidden harmony within the opposites in culture is the symbol. Cassirer says: "It is symbolic thought which overcomes the natural inertia of man and endows him with a new ability, the ability constantly to reshape his human universe."[130] What appears as a struggle between opposing forces in culture is also a manifestation of a harmony originating from the same factor functioning in each. The fact that there is a hidden harmony of connections among all the opposites within cultural activity makes possible a dialectical presentation of culture as a totality by philosophy. In this presentation, philosophy should not gloss over the reality of these oppositions in culture. Cassirer says: "If we wish to grasp its real meaning and import, we must choose not the epic manner of description but the dramatic. For we are confronted, not with a peaceful development of concepts or theories, but with a clash between conflicting spiritual powers."[131]

Cassirer's philosophy of symbolic forms is unique in contemporary philosophy because it shows myth to be a form of thought. No other contemporary philosophy contains a fully expressed theory of myth. All of human culture originates in myth. On Cassirer's conception of myth as a symbolic form, myth contains its own spatial and temporal ordering, based on the division between the sacred and the profane. Myth also employs the same categories of thought that are present in theoretical thought but with a different specific "tonality" (*Tönung*). The category of cause, for example, is present in myth, as based on the constant conjunction of one thing or event with another. Because a

---

129 Cassirer, *Essay*, 222–23.
130 Ibid., 62.
131 Ibid., 9.

certain bird or animal always arrives in the spring, it is seen as the bringer of the spring. In contrast, in theoretical or scientific thought, an analysis of nature is made such that only certain things or events can be considered as the cause of certain other things or events. But, as Cassirer shows, all forms of knowledge arise and develop themselves from mythical thought.

Each symbolic form of culture has within it the urge to dominate culture itself, in the way that myth originally dominates all human activity. Philosophy has the normative role—to put forth the ideal of *harmonia*. It is a role that only the philosophic spirit can assume, because philosophy is not a symbolic form in competition with the other symbolic forms. Philosophy does not make culture. It makes, for us, a knowledge of culture, without which culture cannot be the self-knowledge of the human being writ large, as a whole.

20

Whitehead's Actual Entities

Alfred North Whitehead (1861-1947) was born at Ramsgate on the Isle of Thanet, in the northeast end of Kent, southeast England. In 1880 he went to Trinity College, Cambridge University, to study mathematics. In 1884 he was elected to a fellowship at Trinity and lectured on mathematics. From 1900 to 1911 he collaborated with Bertrand Russell on *Principia Mathematica*, which sought to prove that mathematics could be derived from premises of formal logic. He resigned his lectureship at Cambridge in 1910 and moved to a position at the University of London. He accepted a chair in philosophy at Harvard University in 1924.

At Harvard he developed his philosophy of science into a metaphysical system. He presented *Science and the Modern World* as the Lowell Lectures at Harvard in 1925, followed by his masterwork, *Process and Reality: An Essay on Cosmology* (1929). A third work, *Adventures of Ideas* (1933), completed the center of his philosophy. These works are supplemented by a number of short works. Among them are *Religion in the Making* (1926), *The Function of Reason* (1929), *The Aims of Education* (1929), and *Modes of Thought* (1938). Whitehead died in Cambridge, Massachusetts, in 1947. As of this writing, the first two volumes have appeared of a planned multi-volume, complete critical edition of Whitehead's lectures, writings, and correspondence. Although Hegel is not a source for Whitehead, Whitehead's concept of process and his use of speculative reason has an affinity with Hegel's sense of the self-development of consciousness and the logic of the speculative sentence.

In the first chapter of *Process and Reality*, Whitehead says: "The study of philosophy is a voyage towards the larger generalities."[132] He also says: "Philosophy destroys its usefulness when it indulges in brilliant feats of explaining away."[133] His voyage toward larger generalities and his refusal to indulge in feats of explaining away has its center in one idea—that of "actual entities." They are, he says, "the final real things of which the world is made up. There is no going behind actual entities to find anything more real. They differ among themselves: God is an actual entity, and so is the most trivial puff of existence in far-off empty space."[134] At the basis of all things is not substance or prime matter in any sense. At the basis of all that there is, is process, an activity of constant self-transformation. Whitehead says of the actual entity: "Its 'being' is constituted by its 'becoming.' This is the 'principle of process.'"[135]

The actual entity is an analogue to the ordinary process by which I become a human self. Whitehead explains this process of the self in a passage in *Modes of Thought*: "I shape the activities of the environment into a new creation, which is myself at this moment; and yet, as being myself, it is a continuation of the antecedent world. If we stress the role of the environment, this process is causation. If we stress the role of my immediate pattern of active enjoyment, this process is self-creation. If we stress the role of the conceptual anticipation of the future whose existence is a necessity in the nature of the present, this process is the teleological aim at some ideal in the future."[136] The creation of the human self is always a process of past, present, and future—that of which the Muses originally sing. Past, present, and future are the terms of self-knowledge. A human self is an actual entity writ large.

Whitehead's second, unique cosmological concept is what he calls "prehension." He says: "Every prehension consists of three

---

132 Whitehead, *Process and Reality*, 14.
133 Ibid., 25.
134 Ibid., 27–28.
135 Ibid., 34–35.
136 Whitehead, *Modes of Thought*, 228.

factors: (a) the 'subject' which is prehending, namely, the actual entity in which that prehension is a concrete element; (b) the 'datum' which is prehended; (c) the 'subjective form' which is *how* that subject prehends that datum."[137] Prehension is the primal act that makes possible the conscious act of apprehension of an object. Actual entities have a mental and a physical pole. When an actual entity prehends an idea it is an instance of "conceptual prehension"; when an actual entity reacts to the presence of another actual entity that is for it a datum, it is an instance of "physical prehension." Physical prehensions make up the content of the physical pole of an actual entity; conceptual prehensions make up the content of the mental pole. Whitehead calls this process of incorporating data into the life of an actual entity "concrescence."

Whitehead's theories of actual entities and prehensions are connected to a third theory, that of eternal objects. The theory of eternal objects is intended to account for what is universal in experience. They are Plato's ideas, or the categories of the understanding put forth by Kant. Whitehead says that "an eternal object can be described only in terms of its potentiality for 'ingression' into the becoming of actual entities; and that its analysis only discloses other eternal objects. It is a pure potential."[138] The actual entities are particulars. Eternal objects are universals. By conceiving universals as eternal objects, and their function as pure potentiality, Whitehead intends to avoid the Platonic problem of how the forms, as immaterial substances, participate in things as material substances. Universals, as eternal objects, ingress into the process of the self-development of actual entities.

The universal is a potential to be realized in the activity of an actual entity. Whitehead says: "An eternal object is always a potentiality for actual entities; but in itself, as conceptually felt, it is neutral as to the fact of its physical ingression in any particular

---

137 Whitehead, *Process and Reality*, 35.
138 Ibid., 34.

actual entity of the temporal world."[139] The aim of a particular actual entity, in attaching itself to the universality of the eternal object, is an attempt to be more than a fleeting existent. Every actual entity is seeking being, in the sense of achieving its own immortality. Nothing is purely given for an actual entity. An actual entity desires to terminate its becoming in the being of all that there is. Whitehead says: "The actual entity terminates its becoming in the complex feeling involving a completely determinate bond with every item in the universe, the bond being either a positive or a negative prehension. This termination is the 'satisfaction' of the actual entity."[140]

An actual entity has no nature that is given to it. Whitehead says: "This is the doctrine of the emergent unity of the superject. An actual entity is to be conceived both as a subject, presiding over its own immediacy of becoming, and a superject, which is the atomic creature exercising its function of objective immortality."[141] The actual entity as developing subject aims at objectively being something—a superject. The actual entity makes itself what it is both by positively prehending what it wishes to be and by negatively prehending what it wishes to exclude from its being. When an actual entity is finished with the process of becoming a superject, which includes the ingression of eternal objects, it attains the peace of its satisfaction. Whitehead says: "It has become a 'being'; and it belongs to the nature of every 'being' that it is a potential for every 'becoming.'"[142] The being of every actual entity is potentially an occasion for the prehension and hence the becoming of every other actual entity.

The natural death of an actual entity is the point at which it ceases to be a subject in the process of its own making and becomes the superject of its own making, achieved through its combination of its positive and negative prehensions. Whitehead

---

139 Ibid., 70.
140 Ibid., 71.
141 Ibid.
142 Ibid.

says: "This doctrine, that the final 'satisfaction' of an actual entity is intolerant of any addition, expresses the fact that every actual entity—since it is what it is—is finally its own reason for what it omits."[143] The actuality of an entity's own death becomes a potentiality for the prehension of the becoming of the universe of actual entities at that moment. Since the superject is more than a fleeting state of the subject, it requires the universality of the eternal object to be realized in it. Sheer particularity offers no meaning and hence offers no possibility of satisfaction. The actual entity as subject that has become superject merges its being with all else that is.

Whitehead's cosmology is ultimately a portrait of the self, speaking to itself about the self. Constantly, throughout *Process and Reality*, there is a search for a way to put this speech into words. The terms which initially appear only technical come to take on a life of their own. But it is a language that can be spoken only to those who have crossed the threshold of Whitehead's speculative reason.

Whitehead says: "The Greeks have bequeathed to us two figures, whose real or mythical lives conform to these two notions—Plato and Ulysses. The one shares Reason with the Gods, the other shares it with the foxes."[144] Ulysses's reason is that of the twists and turns of problem-solving. Whitehead's reason is the reason of Plato, the narrative of what it means to be. *Process and Reality* is a likely story of the nature of things. Whitehead says: "The safest general characterization of the European philosophical tradition is that it consists of a series of footnotes to Plato."[145] Philosophy is always a twice-told tale.

---

143 Ibid.
144 Whitehead, *The Function of Reason*, 10.
145 Whitehead, *Process and Reality*, 63.

Epilogue: Ancients and Moderns

The philosophic spirit takes its shape in words—spoken, written, and read. Philosophy, like poetry, is part of world literature. Philosophy as spoken is to be found among the Ancients—Socrates's exchanges in the *agora*, Plato's lectures in the Academy, Aristotle's conversations under the *peripatos* in the Lyceum, Epicurus's teaching in his Garden.

The Moderns introduce the image of the philosopher as the solitary thinker. We find Descartes writing out his ideas in the stove-heated room (*"dans un poêle"*) in Ulm, prompting Miguel de Unamuno to call Descartes's *Discours* a "stove-discourse" (*"discurso de estufa"*).[146] Kant lives in isolation in Königsberg, following events in the rest of the world through newspapers and monthly publications. His response to the Lisbon earthquake of 1755, which called into question, throughout Europe, the belief in God's benevolence, was to write three scientific studies on the causes of earthquakes. Voltaire's response was to write *Candide* (1759), his satirical treatment of the view that "this is the best of all possible worlds."

Philosophy for the Ancients was a way of speaking that could be accompanied by written texts tied to a way of life. Philosophy for the Moderns is a way of research and investigation, not requiring a particular way of life. As Pierre Hadot says, in *What is Ancient Philosophy?*: "A profound difference exists between the representations which the ancients made of *philosophia* and the representation which is usually made of philosophy today."[147] Philosophy, as we find it in Socrates, and in all the schools of Athens, does not exist today. But it is there in memory.

Among the Moderns, Vico offers us an example of a way to balance the memory of the Ancients and the presence of the

---

146 Unamuno, *Tragic Sense of Life*, 35.
147 Hadot, *What is Ancient Philosophy?*, 2.

Moderns. In his autobiography, Vico describes a method of reading that he devised in order to educate himself while he served as tutor to the children of the Rocca family, in their castle in the mountainous region of the Cilento, a three-day carriage ride south from Naples. He had the good fortune to find, in this remote region, an extensive library of the Minor Friars Observants. He undertook a program of reading, to move away from the Baroque manner of poetry (*barocchismo*), to which he had been attracted, and which promotes "an exercise of the mind in feats of wit, which affords pleasure only through falsehood so extravagantly presented as to surprise the right expectations of its hearers."[148]

Vico says: "On successive days he would study Cicero side by side with Boccaccio, Virgil with Dante, and Horace with Petrarca, being curious to see and to judge for himself the differences between them." Vico read these writers "always three times each on the following plan: the first time to grasp each composition as a whole, the second to note the transitions and sequence of things, the third in greater detail to collect the fine turns of thought and expression."[149] Vico's threefold method of reading is a transposition of the three principles of composition in Quintilian's *Institutio oratoria* and that are present throughout classical rhetoric: *inventio* (the collection of materials), *dispositio* (their arrangement and ordering), and *elocutio* (their formulation in language). Oral presentation requires the addition of *memoria* (placement in memory) and *pronuntiatio* (delivery) (3.3). Vico's method of reading converts the three principles of composition into his three principles of comprehension. He looks first for the overall sense of the work, then to its coherence—to the way in which its specific points are ordered—and finally to the way what is said, is said.

Having accomplished his own education by his own lights, Vico found himself in Naples to be "a stranger in his own land."

---

148 Vico, *Autobiography*, 118.
149 Ibid., 120.

Those around him followed only the latest doctrines, having no use for the great ideas of the past and even being derisive of them. Aristotle had become a laughingstock and the great thinkers of the sixteenth century who had revived the ideas of the Ancients were of no interest. Philosophy had become no more than the promotion of contemporary doctrines. Philosophy had lost its connection with the spirit of humane letters governed by the Muses, having no concern for eloquence. Vico realized that he must, on his own, determine what sources could serve as guides for his own thought.

He first chose Plato and Tacitus as his guides, because "Tacitus contemplates man as he is, Plato as he should be. . . . The wise man should be formed both of esoteric wisdom such as Plato's and of common wisdom such as that of Tacitus." Vico later added, to Plato the philosopher and Tacitus the historian, Francis Bacon, "a man of incomparable wisdom both common and esoteric, at one and the same time a universal man in theory and in practice." Bacon is a modern synthesis of Vico's two Ancients. Vico says he "now proposed to have these three unique authors ever before him in meditation and writing."[150]

While proceeding with his thought guided by these three figures, Vico accepted a commission to write the life of the military figure, Marshal Antonio Carafa (1646–1693). In preparing this work, Vico discovered Hugo Grotius's *De iure belli ac pacis* (*On the Law of War and Peace*) (1625). Grotius's work is the first major exposition of the conception of a system of international and natural law. In Grotius, Vico says: "He found a fourth author to add to the three he had before himself." He says: "Plato adorns rather than confirms his esoteric wisdom with the common wisdom of Homer." Tacitus, Vico says, "intersperses his metaphysics, ethics and politics with the facts, as they have come down to him from the times, scattered and confused and without system." Among the Moderns, "Bacon sees that the sum of human

---

150 Ibid., 138–39.

and divine knowledge of his time needs supplementing and emending."[151]

But Vico says that Bacon, unlike Grotius, does not provide a complete conception of human law. Thus Vico supplements the achievements of Bacon with Grotius, who "embraces in a system of universal law the whole of philosophy and philology, including both parts of the latter, the history on the one hand of facts and events, both fabulous and real, and on the other of the three languages, Hebrew, Greek and Latin; that is to say, the three learned languages of antiquity that have been handed down to us by the Christian religion."[152] As Plato and Tacitus have supplemented each other, Bacon and Grotius supplement each other.

Vico shows us that to pursue philosophy, we need to place before us a set of four figures to act as sources and guides. Four is the number of internal opposition and enclosure—the four points on a compass, the four quarter-hours on a clock, the four types of propositions in logic on the Traditional Square of Opposition, and the sequence of three tragedies plus a satyr-play in ancient Greek theater. Vico's fourfold of authors is reminiscent of the ancient problem of squaring the circle that is as old as Anaxagoras and pursued by many, including Cusanus, until the modern mathematician, Ferdinand von Lindeman, by proving that π is not a transcendental number, showed that the circle cannot be squared. Vico does not attempt to subduct his own views from the square of his four authors. Instead he encircles his sources with his sense of *corso* and *ricorso*.

Speculative philosophy takes thought in a circle. The final principle at which such thought arrives is always already present in primary form in the beginning. In the *Metaphysics*, Aristotle says: "The body which moves in a circle is eternal and unresting" (1093a). The circle is the form of continuous and perfect motion. Hegel says that his system is a circle, and that moreover, it is a

---

[151] Ibid., 155.
[152] Ibid.

circle of circles (*ein Kreis von Kreisen*). Each moment of his system returns to its own beginning and is then the beginning of the next moment. Hegel says: "The true is the becoming of itself, the circle that presupposes its end as its goal, and has its end as its beginning, and is only actual through implementation and its end."[153]

It is impractical to attempt to work from the whole of the history of philosophy at once, although a knowledge of the history of philosophy as a whole is necessary in order to seek out one's sources and guides. It is too narrow simply to settle on a figure or school of thought and become a follower of that form of philosophy. It is not especially difficult to find two or three source-authors. It is quite difficult to secure a fourth. As Vico's account suggests, the set of four authors must come together over time. Once we have determined our own four authors, the circle of our thought can move around them. They serve as master *topoi* from which to think our own thoughts.

In the method of reading that Vico devised, he brought together the Latins, Cicero, Virgil, and Horace, with the Tuscans, Boccaccio, Dante, and Petrarca. For the composition of his works, he brought together the two Ancients, Plato and Tacitus, with the two Moderns, Bacon and Grotius. This balancing of Ancients and Moderns appears in his oration on education, *De nostri temporis studiorum ratione* (*On the Study Methods of Our Time*). Vico says that we Moderns "have discovered many things of which the Ancients were entirely ignorant; the Ancients, on the other hand, knew much still unknown to us."[154] To think well we must move between these two great sources, not placing one over the other. The philosophic spirit is present in both.

James Joyce—who based *Finnegans Wake* on Vico's *Scienza nuova*—told the French literary critic, Jacques Mercanton, who asked Joyce about the nature of his talent and method: "Chance furnishes me what I need. I am like a man who stumbles along;

---

153 Hegel, *Phenomenology*, par. 18.
154 Vico, *Study Methods*, 4.

my foot strikes something, I bend over, and it is exactly what I want."[155] Of Vico, we might say the same. It is by chance that Vico finds himself with access to the library of the Minor Friars Observants in the Cilento. It is chance that Vico is given the commission to write the life of Antonio Carafa and, in his preparation for it, to discover Grotius, his fourth author. When the mind is set on a course to pursue wisdom, taking advantage of what chance provides is always the decisive act.

---

155 Mercanton, "James Joyce," 213.

Works Cited

Anselm, Saint. *Proslogium*. In *Saint Anselm: Basic Writings*, 1–34. Translated by S. W. Deane. La Salle, IL: Open Court, 1962.

Blackwood, Stephen. *The "Consolation" of Boethius as Poetic Liturgy.* Oxford: Oxford University Press, 2015.

Bloch, Enid. "Hemlock Poisoning and the Death of Socrates." In Thomas C. Brickhouse and Nicholas D. Smith, *The Trial and Execution of Socrates: Sources and Controversies*, 255–72. New York: Oxford, 2002.

Brecht, Bertolt. *Flüchtlingsgespräche*. Berlin: Suhrkamp, 1961.

Bruno, Giordano. *Cause, Principle and Unity*. Translated by Robert de Lucca. Cambridge: Cambridge University Press, 1998.

———. *On the Infinite Universe and Worlds*. In Dorothea Waley Singer, *Giordano Bruno: His Life and Thought*, 225–378. Translated by Dorothea Waley Singer. New York: Schuman, 1950.

Cassirer, Ernst. "Der Begriff der symbolische Form im Aufbau der Geisteswissenschaften." In Vol. 16 of Ernst Cassirer, *Gesammelte Werke Hamburger Ausgabe*, 75–104. Edited by Birgit Recki. Hamburg: Meiner, 2003.

———. *An Essay on Man: An Introduction to a Philosophy of Human Culture*. New Haven: Yale University Press, 1944.

———. *The Individual and the Cosmos in Renaissance Philosophy*. Translated By Mario Domandi. New York: Harper, 1963.

———. *The Myth of the State*. New Haven: Yale University Press, 1946.

———. *The Philosophy of Symbolic Forms*. Translated by Ralph Manheim. 3 vols. New Haven: Yale University Press, 1953–1957.

———. *The Philosophy of Symbolic Forms: The Metaphysics of Symbolic Forms*. Vol. 4. Edited by John Michael Krois and Donald Phillip Verene. Translated by John Michael Krois. New Haven: Yale University Press, 1996.

———. *The Problem of Knowledge: Philosophy, Science, and History since Hegel*. Translated by William H. Woglom and Charles W. Hendel. New Haven: Yale University Press, 1950.

———. *The Question of Jean-Jacques Rousseau*. Translated by Peter Gay. Bloomington: Indiana University Press, 1963.

Copleston, Frederick. *A History of Philosophy*. Vol. 7. London: Burns and Oates, 1968.

Descartes, René. *Oeuvres*. Edited by Charles Adam and Paul Tannery. 11 vols. Paris: Vrin, 1996.

———. *The Philosophical Writings of Descartes*. Translated by John Cottingham, Robert Stoothoff, Dugald Murdoch, and Anthony Kenny. 3 vols. Cambridge: Cambridge University Press, 1994.

Digest of Justinian. Translated by Alan Watson. Vol. 1. Philadelphia: University of Pennsylvania Press, 1985.

Eco, Umberto. *Kant and the Platypus: Essays on Language and Cognition*. Translated by Alastair McEwen. San Diego: Harcourt,1999.

Findlay, J. N. "Foreword." In G. W. F. Hegel, *Phenomenology of Spirit*, v-xxx. Translated by A. V. Miller. Oxford: Clarendon, 1977.

Frankfort, Henri and H. A. Frankfort. "The Emancipation of Thought from Myth." In Henri Frankfort, H. A. Frankfort, John A. Wilson, Thorkild Jacobsen, and William A. Irwin, *The Intellectual Adventure of Ancient Man: An Essay on Speculative Thought in the Ancient Near East*, 363–87. Chicago: University of Chicago Press, 1977.

Greek Mathematical Works. Translated by Ivor Thomas. 2 vols. Cambridge: Harvard University Press, 2000.

Hadot, Pierre. *What is Ancient Philosophy?* Translated by Michael Chase. Cambridge: Harvard University Press, 2002.

Hartshorne, Charles. "Introduction to the Second Edition." In *SaintAnselm: Basic Writings*, 1–19. Translated by S. W. Deane. LaSalle, IL: Open Court, 1962.

Hegel, G. W. F. *The Phenomenology of Spirit*. Translated by Michael Inwood. Oxford: Oxford University Press, 2018.

———. *Vorlesungen über die Geschichte der Philosophie*. Vol. 19 of G. W. F. Hegel, *Werke*. Edited by Eva Moldenhauer and Karl Markus Michel.Frankfurt am Main: Suhrkamp, 1971.

Hobbes, Thomas. *Leviathan*. Edited by C. B. Macpherson. New York: Penguin, 1968.

Homer. *The Iliad*. Translated by Robert Fagles. New York: Penguin, 1990.

———. *The Odyssey*. Translated by Robert Fagles. New York: Penguin, 1996.

Joyce, James. "The Day of the Rabblement." In *The Critical Writings of James Joyce*, 68–72. Edited by Ellsworth Mason and Richard Ellmann. New York: Viking, 1959.

Kant, Immanuel. *Critique of Pure Reason*. Translated by Norman Kemp Smith. London: Macmillan, 1958.

———. *Groundwork of the Metaphysic of Morals*. Translated by H. J. Paton. New York: Harper, 2009.

Klinke, Willibald. *Kant for Everyman*. Translated by Michael Bullock. New York: Collier, 1962.

Laks, André, and Glenn W. Most, eds. *Early Greek Philosophy*. Vol. 5, Pt. 2. Cambridge: Harvard University Press, 2016.

Lewis, Charlton T., and Charles Short. *A Latin Dictionary*. Oxford: Clarendon, 1980.

Liddell, Henry George, and Robert Scott. *A Greek–English Lexicon*. Oxford: Clarendon, 1968.

Mercanton, Jacques. "The Hours of James Joyce." In *Portraits of the Artist in Exile: Recollections of James Joyce by Europeans*, 206–52. Edited by Willard Potts. New York: Harcourt, 1986.

Mill, John Stuart. *Utilitarianism*. Edited by George Sher. Indianapolis: Hackett, 2001.

Montaigne, Michel de. *Essais*. Edited by Maurice Rat. 3 vols. Paris: Garnier, 1958.

Nicholas of Cusa. *Nicholas of Cusa on Learned Ignorance*. Translated by Jasper Hopkins. Minneapolis: Arthur J. Banning Press, 1985.

Niermeyer, J. F., and C. van de Kieft. *Mediae Latinitatis Lexicon Minus*. 2 vols. Leiden: Brill, 2002.

Pico della Mirandola, Giovanni. "Oration on the Dignity of Man." In Ernst Cassirer, Paul Oskar Kristeller, and John Hermann Randall, Jr., eds. *The Renaissance Philosophy of Man*, 223–54. Translated by Elizabeth Livermore Forbes. Chicago: University of Chicago Press, 1967.

Pope, Alexander. "An Essay on Man." In *Pope Poems*, 193–221. Edited by Claude Rawson. New York: Knopf, 2018.

The Pythagorean Sourcebook and Library. Translated by Kenneth Sylvan Guthrie. Grand Rapids, MI: Phanes Press, 1988.

Rousseau, Jean-Jacques. *The First and Second Discourses*. Translated by Roger D. Masters and Judith R. Masters. New York: St. Martin's, 1964.

———. *Oeuvres Complètes*. 4 vols. Paris: Gallimard, 1959.

Santayana, George. *Three Philosophical Poets: Lucretius, Dante, Goethe*. Vol. 6 of *The Works of George Santayana*, Triton Edition. New York: Scribner's, 1936.

Snell, Bruno. *The Discovery of the Mind in Greek Philosophy and Literature*. Translated by T. G. Rosenmeyer. New York: Dover, 1982.

Unamuno, Miguel de. *The Tragic Sense of Life in Men and Peoples*. Translated by J. E. Crawford Fitch. London: Macmillan, 1931.

Vico, Giambattista. *The Autobiography of Giambattista Vico*. Translated by Max Harold Fisch and Thomas Goddard Bergin. Ithaca: Cornell University Press, 1990.

———. *Institutiones Oratoriae*. Edited by Giuliano Crifò. Naples: Istituto Suor Benincasa, 1989.

———. Letter to Nicole Gaetari di Laurenzano of March 1732. In *Epistole con aggiunte le epistole dei suoi correspondenti*, 165–66. Edited by Manuela Sanna. Naples: Morano, 1992.

———. *The New Science of Giambattista Vico*. Translated by Thomas Goddard Bergin and Max Harold Fisch. Ithaca: Cornell University Press, 1984.

———. *On the Study Methods of Our Time*. Translated by Elio Gianturco. Ithaca: Cornell University Press, 1990.

Vives, Juan Luis. "A Fable about Man." In Ernst Cassirer, Paul Oskar Kristeller, and John Hermann Randall, Jr., eds. *The Renaissance Philosophy of Man*, 387–93. Translated by Nancy Lenkeith. Chicago: University of Chicago Press, 1967.

Whitehead, Alfred North. *The Function of Reason*. Boston: Beacon, 1962.

———. *Modes of Thought*. New York: Capricorn, 1958.

———. *Process and Reality: An Essay on Cosmology*. New York: Harper, 1960.

Yates, Frances A. *Giordano Bruno and the Hermetic Tradition*. Chicago: University of Chicago Press, 1991.

Yeats, W. B. "Among School Children." In *Modern Poems: An Introduction to Poetry*, 46–48. Edited by Richard Ellmann and Robert O'Clair. New York: Norton, 1976.

Index

Achilles, 27, 98
Agamemnon, 27
Alembert, Jean Le Rond d', 114
Anaxagoras, 71
Anselm, Saint, 82
   ontological argument, 73-76
Antisthenes, 31
Apollo, 21, 28, 40
Archimedes, 88-90
Aristotle, 28, 41, 69, 133
   on circular motion, 134
   on Empedocles, 40
   on ethics, 57-61
   on imitation, 15
   on metaphor, 14
   on Thales, 32-34
   on wonder, 12-13
Asclepius, 41, 57
Athena, 41
Augustine, Saint, 90

Bacon, Francis, 95, 133-34
Boccaccio, Giovanni, 69, 135
Boethius, 69
   concept of consolation, 69-72
Brecht, Bertolt, 117
Bruno, Giordano, 81
   concept of infinite worlds, 81-84

Cassirer, Ernst, 14
   on Cusanus, 77
   on Rousseau's *Discourse*, 103
   on self-knowledge, 24
   on symbolic forms, 119-24
   on Vico's view of myth, 96-97
Cebes, 46

Chaerephon, 20
Chaucer, Geoffrey, 69
Christina, Queen of Sweden, 87
Cicero, 69, 132, 135
   concept of philosophy, 11-12
   on Lucretius, 64
   on Pythagoras, 37
   on Socrates, 45, 47
   on Thales, 32
Cohen, Hermann, 119
Colvius, Andreas, 90
Copernicus, Nicolas, 84
Copleston, Frederick, 15
Crito, 29
Cusanus. *See* Nicholas of Cusa

Dante, 63, 69, 99, 132, 135
Descartes, René, 119, 131
   concept of *cogito*, 87-90
Diderot, Denis, 114
Diodorus Siculus, 89
Diogenes Laertius, 57
   on apotheosis of Empedocles, 42
   on charge against Socrates, 45
   on Epicurus's view of death, 65
   on origin of word "philosopher," 36-38
   on Plato, 52
   on Thales, 31
Diotima, 13-14

Echecrates, 45
Eco, Umberto, 110
Empedocles, 39-42, 63
Epicurus, 64-66, 131
Epimetheus, 102
Eros, 13-14
Euthyphro, 49

142 INDEX

Fichte, Johann Gottlieb, 113
Findlay, John, 114
Frankfort, Henri, and H. A., 23
Frederick, Crown Prince, 107

Galileo, 87, 91, 96
Goethe, Johann Wolfgang von, 63
Grotius, Hugo, 133–36

Hadot, Pierre, 131
Hartshorne, Charles, 73
Hegel, Georg Wilhelm Friedrich, 113
  on Anselm, 76
  comparison with Whitehead, 125
  concept of speculation, 113–17
  system as a circle, 134-35
Hephestus, 101
Heraclides of Pontus, 37, 42
Heraclitus, 122-23
Hermes Trismegistus, 81
Herodotus, 31, 33
Hesiod, 13, 27–28, 30, 71
Hippocrates, 41
Hobbes, Thomas, 96
  and Book of Job, 93–94
  concept of the state, 92–94
Homer, 27, 35, 133
  founder of Greek culture, 51–53, 55
  use of similes, 40–41
Horace, 11, 132, 135

Iamblichus, 35

Jove. See Zeus
Joyce, James, 84, 135

Jupiter. See Zeus

Kant, Immanuel, 127, 131
  and Cassirer, 120
  categorical imperative, 57–58
  concept of perfect island, 110–12
  theory of the schematism, 109–11

Leon (ruler of Phlius), 37-38
Lindeman, Ferdinand von, 134
Lucretius, 82
  his poem, 63–66

Mallarmé, Stéphane, 114
Marcellus, 89
Mercanton, Jacques, 135
Mersenne, Marin, 91
Mill, John Stuart, 57–58
Mnemosyne, 28, 30, 97
Montaigne, Michel Eyquem de, 24
Musaeus, 27
Muses, 20, 27
  and Boethius, 71
  individual identities, 28–30
  and Vico, 97, 100

Newton, Isaac, 96
Nicholas of Cusa, 82
  concept of learned ignorance, 77–80

Odysseus. See Ulysses
Orpheus, 27
Ovid, 105

Pausanias, 42

Phaedo, 45–46
Phaedrus, 19, 28, 41
Pico della Mirandola, Giovanni, 21–23
Petrarca, Francesco, 132, 135
Plato, 12–13, 19–20, 35, 69, 127
  Cassirer's view of Platonic forms, 120
  on Homer, 27, 53, 55
  Platonic Academy, 28, 37, 51, 57, 131
  on poetry, 51–55
  on pre-Socratics, 23
  and Prometheus legend, 102
  setting of *Phaedo*, 45
  as source for Vico, 133–34
  speculative manner of philosophy, 117, 129
  and wording in *Apology*, 47
Plautus, 77
Plutarch, 20–21, 89
Pope, Alexander, 24
Porphyry, 35–36, 69
Prometheus, 102, 104
Pythagoras, 35–38, 45–46

Quintilian, 132

Rimbaud, Arthur, 114
Rousseau, Jean-Jacques, 101
  his moral philosophy, 101–5
Russell, Bertrand, 125

Santayana, George, 63
Schelling, Friedrich Wilhelm Joseph von, 113
Seven Sages, 20, 31
Shakespeare, William, 114
Simmias, 46
Socrates, 20, 41, 87, 103, 131
  and Cusanus's concept of ignorance, 77
  and death, 27, 42, 45–46
  Diotima's speech on Eros, 13–14
  method of philosophy, 45–49
  and Muses, 28–30
  and Plato's quarrel with poets, 52–55
  and self-knowledge, 19
  on Thales, 33
  and wonder, 12
Solon, 20, 32, 51

Tacitus, 133–34
Thales, 20, 31–34
Theaetetus, 12, 30
Theodorus, 33
Thucydides, 91
Tzetzes, John, 89

Ulysses, 41, 98, 129
Unamuno, Miguel de, 131

Vico, Giambattista, 95
  compares Boethius with Plato, 72
  interpretation of Solon, 32
  method of reading and writing, 131–36
  theory of poetic wisdom, 95–100
Virgil, 132, 135
Vives, Juan Luis, 22–23
Voltaire, François Marie Arouet, 131

Walton, Francis R., 89
Whitehead, Alfred North, 14
  theory of actual entities, 125–29

Wilde, Oscar, 117

Xenophon, 46

Yates, Frances, 81
Yeats, William Butler, 35-36

Zeno, 71
Zeus, 22, 27–29, 98, 102

ibidem.eu